THE PSYCHOLOGY OF BELONGING

Can a sense of belonging increase life satisfaction? Why do we sometimes feel lonely? How can we sustain lasting human connections?

The Psychology of Belonging explores why feeling like we belong is so important throughout our lives, from childhood to old age, irrespective of culture, race or geography. With its virtues and shortcomings, belonging to groups such as families, social groups, schools, workplaces and communities is fundamental to our identity and wellbeing, even in a time when technology has changed the way we connect with each other.

In a world where loneliness and social isolation is on the rise, *The Psychology of Belonging* shows how meaningful connections can build a sense of belonging for all of us.

Kelly-Ann Allen is an internationally recognised belonging researcher and psychologist at Monash University and the University of Melbourne. She is a codirector and founder of the International Belonging Research Laboratory.

THE PSYCHOLOGY OF EVERYTHING

People are fascinated by psychology, and what makes humans tick. Why do we think and behave the way we do? We've all met armchair psychologists claiming to have the answers, and people that ask if psychologists can tell what they're thinking. The Psychology of Everything is a series of books which debunk the popular myths and pseudo-science surrounding some of life's biggest questions.

The series explores the hidden psychological factors that drive us, from our subconscious desires and aversions, to our natural social instincts. Absorbing, informative, and always intriguing, each book is written by an expert in the field, examining how research-based knowledge compares with popular wisdom, and showing how psychology can enrich our understanding of modern life.

Applying a psychological lens to an array of topics and contemporary concerns – from sex, to fashion, to conspiracy theories – The Psychology of Everything will make you look at everything in a new way.

Titles in the series:

The Psychology of Gender
Gary Wood

The Psychology of Climate
    Change
Geoffrey Beattie and Laura McGuire

The Psychology of Vampires
David Cohen

The Psychology of Chess
Fernand Gobet

The Psychology of Music
Susan Hallam

The Psychology of Weather
Trevor Harley

The Psychology of Driving
Graham J. Hole

The Psychology of Retirement
Doreen Rosenthal and Susan
    M. Moore

The Psychology of School
    Bullying
Peter Smith

The Psychology of Celebrity
Gayle Stever

The Psychology of Dog
    Ownership
Craig Roberts and Theresa Barlow

The Psychology of Social Media
Ciarán Mc Mahon

The Psychology of Happiness
Peter Warr

The Psychology of Politics
Barry Richards

The Psychology of the
    Paranormal
David Groome

The Psychology of Prejudice
Richard Gross

The Psychology of Intelligence
Sonja Falck

The Psychology of Terrorism
Neil Shortland

The Psychology of Dreaming
Josie Malinowski

The Psychology of Exercise
Josephine Perry

The Psychology of Video Games
Celia Hodent

The Psychology of Religion
Vassilis Saroglou

The Psychology of Belonging
Kelly-Ann Allen

For further information about this series please visit www.routledge
textbooks.com/textbooks/thepsychologyofeverything/

THE PSYCHOLOGY OF BELONGING

KELLY-ANN ALLEN

Routledge
Taylor & Francis Group

LONDON AND NEW YORK

First published 2021
by Routledge
2 Park Square, Milton Park, Abingdon, Oxon OX14 4RN

and by Routledge
52 Vanderbilt Avenue, New York, NY 10017

Routledge is an imprint of the Taylor & Francis Group, an informa business

British Library Cataloguing-in-Publication Data
A catalogue record for this book is available from the British Library

Library of Congress Cataloging-in-Publication Data
A catalog record for this book has been requested

ISBN: 978-0-367-34753-6 (hbk)
ISBN: 978-0-367-34752-9 (pbk)
ISBN: 978-0-429-32768-1 (ebk)

Typeset in Joanna
by Apex CoVantage, LLC

This book is lovingly dedicated to my children: Henry, Florence, and Georgie.

Kelly-Ann Allen

CONTENTS

FOREWORD

As 2020 dawned in Melbourne, Australia, an exhibition at our National Gallery of Victoria displayed the work of internationally renowned contemporary American artist KAWS, aka Brian Donnell, in an exhibition titled KAWS: Companionship in the Age of Loneliness. While there is humour in the works, they reflect pathos, hope and humanity, recognising that loneliness is an experience that resonates with so many. Indeed, the creative works reflect the needs of our time to connect and belong. Dr Kelly-Ann Allen, a scholarly researcher, focuses on these important elements in her highly readable volume *The Psychology of Belonging*. The first months of 2020 also brought with them the outbreak of the COVID-19 pandemic that swept the world and forced major populations to isolate as countries like Australia, the UK and the US went into lockdown. Schools closed, and young people were separated from their friends for extended periods. Both of these events bring home the significance of understanding loneliness and isolation and its antithesis, belonging: the cure that can make the difference. Dr Allen has been researching this field for a decade and manages to capture in this volume both the history and the contemporary world of young people as they establish their connections through technology, with its strengths and its pitfalls. The volume covers childhood through adolescence and into adulthood. It is sufficiently comprehensive to address both the virtues and the shortcomings of belonging, covering topics such as inclusiveness, rejection, cults and terrorism. Chapter 7 treats the reader to ways of building belonging. Sound psychological underpinnings are embedded in this volume, which both informs and guides us to a better place.

Erica Frydenberg, PhD
2 April 2020

PREFACE

Research into school shootings, radicalisation, mental illness, chronic loneliness, social isolation and suicide have one thing in common: an inverse relationship with belonging. Examining our need to belong has never been more important as we strive to tackle some of the most complex social issues of our time.

Loneliness is one of the most burgeoning problems faced by modern societies. Numerous global studies report that we are facing an international loneliness epidemic. Government intervention and public awareness are gaining momentum in Australia, the UK and elsewhere. The number of people over 50 experiencing loneliness will reach two million in the UK by 2026. The political climate is responding. In 2018, the UK appointed a minister for loneliness, and there have been recent calls for other countries around the world to follow the lead.

Academics and activists are calling for proactive and preventive approaches that focus on communities and belonging. There is a need to examine belonging in the context of a social history marked by race, culture and changes to the way we live, work and integrate with others.

As a human species, we share one thing in common: our need to belong. When that need is not met, we can see a devastating impact on the human psyche.

The aim of this book is to present an engaging overview of the psychology of belonging, which draws from theory and research across seven accessible chapters. The chapters will examine belonging through a range of perspectives and highlight why belonging needs to brought to public conversations.

ACKNOWLEDGEMENTS

I acknowledge the dedication and support of Eleanor Reedy and Vilija Stephen from Routledge. They welcomed an idea and helped turn it into a publication. I thank them for recognising the human importance of belonging and for providing a vehicle by which people can learn more about themselves in the context of their day-to-day life. My sincere thanks go to Paul Scade, Sandra Tilbrook, John Allen, Andrew Cox, Phoebe Masallo-Caballo, Ruth Anne Hui Tsien Keh and Charlotte Mapp for their assistance in preparing the manuscript for publication. I am grateful also to Bonnie M. Hagerty, Bruce Perry and Arthur Aron for so generously providing permission to use their measures and figures in the book.

I also acknowledge the many icons, mentors and great researchers in the field of belonging, many of whom are members of the International Belonging Research Laboratory (IBRL). Thank you for your ongoing contributions to belonging research and making this book possible: Mark Leary, Chris Rozek, George M. Slavich, Greg Walton, Erica Frydenberg, Roy F. Baumeister, Michael Furlong, John Hattie, Lea Waters, Kathryn Riley, Dennis McInerney, Christopher D. Slaten, Sue Roffey, DeLeon Gray, Hamid Sharif Nia, Gökmen Arslan, Peggy Kern, Dianne Vella-Brodrick, Annie Gowing, Alan Tilbrook, Jill Fernandes,

Divya Jindal-Snape, Theofilos Gkinopoulos, Chris Boyle, Margaret Costello, Megan Corcoran, Michelle Lim and Tracii Ryan. I also thank my faculty colleagues Gerald Wurf, Alex Whitelock-Wainwright, Andrea Reupert, Christine Grove, Emily Berger and Lefteris Patlamazoglou; graduate students, Roby Vota, Denise Wong, Erin Geary, Kate Fortune, Angela McCahey, Heather Craig, Shaista Shohail, Rebecca Johnson, Ashleigh Parks, Lulu Cheng, Fàtima Canseco López, and social media supporters Rocco Cardamone and Hope Calvert. A special thank-you goes to the industry partners and supporters of the IBRL who provide a voice and pathway for research to reach the people who need it the most: Ruth Thomas Suh, *Reject* documentary, Brendan Bailey, the head of Berry Street Education Model, Berry Street, Stumped, the Faculty of Education, Monash University and Growing Great Schools Worldwide.

Lastly, the book would not have been possible without the love, support and sense of belonging provided by my family. Families are the very first place we learn about belonging, and I am indebted to Rosemary O'Brien, Mark O'Brien, Stuart Allen, John Allen, Diane Allen and my beautiful children, Henry, Florence and Georgie.

1

THE BEGINNINGS
OF BELONGING

Have you ever felt the pang of exclusion? It might have been at school, at work or in a social group. You might have wanted to belong so badly that it hurt. The experience might have sent you searching for answers to explain why you did not fit in. Was it something you did? Was it something you did not do? Was it the other people involved?

The feeling of exclusion or ostracisation can be painful. It can shape our future interactions and our attempts to belong in other social contexts. It can affect our mental health, our wellbeing and even our physical health, because our sense of belonging is fundamental to living our day-to-day lives.

We find much of our meaning, identity, relevance and satisfaction in life through our sense of belonging to groups. At family, community and societal levels, we rely on others for support, validation and understanding. Belonging to groups, whether these be families, groups of friends, social groups, schools, workplaces or communities more broadly, has a positive effect on several key factors that contribute to our successful healthy functioning as human beings in a society.

Our need to belong is like our need for water. We can spend some time ignoring our thirst without any harmful impact, but sooner or later, our body will start to send warning signals that things are out of balance. While the effects of dehydration are more immediately apparent, the effects of not belonging may be less obvious initially, but they are no less important. The serious consequences of a lack of water are well known, but less known are the consequences of a lack of belonging that can contribute to early death – for example, in the case of suicide. Like water, belonging is a fundamental human need, and the lack of it can have a significant detrimental impact on our lives.

This introductory chapter seeks to draw from the broader literature, both academic and popular, in a bid to define and conceptualise belonging in a colourful yet meaningful way. We will spend some time examining evolutionary perspectives and animal studies and will pay homage to the founders of specific psychological theories that have shaped the way we understand what it truly means to belong.

CONTEXTUALISING OUR NEED TO BELONG

What does "belonging" mean to you? Many people relate a sense of belonging to feeling accepted, included, understood, welcomed, liked and appreciated. Academically, belonging is defined as a unique and subjective experience that relates to a yearning for connection with others, the need for positive regard and the desire for interpersonal connection (Rogers, 1951). Belonging is like loneliness in the sense that belonging does not depend on the number of others or groups you surround yourself with. Rather, belonging is a perception or an evaluation of how you feel. This evaluation may relate to the quality of social connections, to their meaning, to a person's satisfaction with them or even to the way someone feels towards a place or an event. The belief that your sense of belonging or level of loneliness relates to the number of people that are around you is a common misconception. It is possible to have numerous social networks, friends and family members but still feel lonely and like you do not belong.

Baumeister and Leary (1995) suggest that a sense of belonging is pervasive and compelling and is something that we continually seek to find and maintain. What implications might this have on the decisions and choices we make in life? Have you ever actively made a life-changing decision that was directed at feeling a sense of belonging somewhere? Sometimes a sense of belonging can drive us to relocate to the other side of the world or to uproot ourselves and return "home" after a period away. Making such decisions might involve leaving behind fragments of your life or giving up other things you value, in a bid to regain or strengthen a sense of belonging. Or perhaps the decision was made for the sake of another. While we all have a need for belonging ourselves, Baumeister and Leary also suggest that we are deeply conditioned to provide a sense of belonging to others. It seems that our sense of belonging is so important to us as a species that it has the potential to shape our relationships with others, groups and even whole communities.

A sense of belonging can be associated with not just people but all manner of things. We know that people commonly report a sense of connection to places, memories, objects, experiences, events, countries, places and land. A sense of belonging can be experiential and linked to certain sounds, smells, textures, tastes and sensations. Senses of belonging are thus complex and dynamic agglomerations that are unique and special to each person. Think about a place where you belong. Are there certain sounds, smells or textures that you associate with belonging to that place? Perhaps there is a smell that takes you back to a specific time in childhood: the scent of a hand cream that your grandmother used to wear or a cooking smell that recalls a special place and time when you felt a sense of belonging? We all have olfactory memories of this type, and triggering them can bring up feelings that may positively or negatively affect how we feel we belong. The same is true for all our other senses. Belonging, then, needs to be understood in a way that recognises this complexity and is not necessarily always defined narrowly in purely interpersonal terms.

Another aspect of belonging that is sometimes discussed in the literature on the subject is that which relates to autonomy, choice and commitment. This dimension of belonging is described by Toko-pa Turner in her book *Belonging*:

> At the very heart of "belonging" is the word "long". To be-long to something is to stay with it for the long haul. It is an active choice we make to a relationship, to a place, to our body, to a life because we value it.
>
> (Turner, 2017, p. 76)

In understanding belonging, it is vital to take account of cross-cultural considerations, because the nuances of the conceptual language of belonging can vary widely across the globe. In Australia, for instance, belonging is core to Indigenous culture and values. The language of kinship is used to describe the value of all relationships, including belonging to the land. In Denmark, people use the treasured word "*fællesskab*", a term not readily translatable into English but which indicates togetherness and strongly associated social bonds.

Some writers have also sought to identify differences in the understanding of belonging between collectivist cultures and individualist cultures. Much of the thought in this space assumes that Western culture is individualistic, whereas Eastern culture (usually referring to East Asia) is collectivistic. On this account, individualist culture is underpinned by the self and the idea of independence, whereas collectivist culture is focused on relationships and communities that function as a collective whole. The paradox here is that when students are asked about the degree to which they feel a sense of belonging to their school, students from collectivist countries tend to rate their sense of belonging much lower than do students from individualist countries (Cortina et al., 2017). What might be going on to explain this apparent divergence from expectations? It may be that Eastern countries have a different way of prioritising belonging. If this is correct, then when we consider belonging in a cultural context, we will have to take account of different valuations as well as different conceptualisations and descriptions.

THE UPS AND DOWNS OF BELONGING

Belonging can be fluid; a person may not always feel that they do or do not belong, and changes can occur either rapidly or comparatively slowly. There might be many things or groups we belong to, and what we belong to may change from week to week. Belonging can be influenced by temporally localised factors, such as the specific interactions you have with others in a given period and the environment in which you find yourself at a given time. Your sense of belonging may even be influenced by rapid sequences of events or stressors that can result in you questioning your belonging more than once during a given day. Consider for a moment whether an event has challenged your sense of belonging to something else in the past. Was it the way someone looked at you? The absence of a chair around the table? Were you left off an email list, or did something happen to make you feel like an imposter at work? Because levels of belonging are affected by such a broad range of factors, an individual's sense of belonging is better understood as being in a state of flux, either rapid or slow-moving, rather than as being static. This is because a sense of belonging is deeply subjective, and our persistent inner drive to belong demands that we regularly reassess and revaluate whether we belong in a given context.

Belonging-related stressors can be more intense for those who identify as belonging to racial minorities, those who identify as sexually or gender diverse or even those who display behaviours, attributes or abilities that deviate from the so-called social norm (see Chapter 4). The differences between belonging and fitting in have been the subject of considerable discussion. Professor Brené Brown writes in her book *The Gifts of Imperfection: Let Go of Who You Think You're Supposed to Be and Embrace Who You Are* that "[f]itting in is about assessing a situation and becoming who you need to be to be accepted. Belonging, on the other hand, doesn't require us to change who we are; it requires us to be who we are" (Brown, 2010, p. 232). She goes on to say that a desire to fit in is, in fact, the opposite of belonging. In fact, other research has found that the desire to "stand out" – that is, striving for distinctiveness from others – actually predicts a sense of belonging (Gray et al., 2019). A desire for uniqueness is common; regardless of whether an individual's sense of belonging is rooted in a collectivist or individualist culture, it may serve as a springboard for a sense of belonging through the development of self-identity/self-concept.

Greg Walton has paid attention to questions concerning belonging in adolescence. He has tested many brief interventions concerned with belonging (see Chapter 2), and the core of his work emphasises that not feeling a sense of belonging is normal and commonly overcome. He suggests that everyone has a feeling of not belonging from time to time and that these feelings can be made worse by the human tendency to identify the negative more easily than the positive – what psychologists call a negative bias. Research into negative bias has examined how our perceptions and attributions can affect the ways we think, feel and behave. The hardwiring that biases us towards the negative can have a deep impact on how we go about our lives. People will be more likely to make a note of all the reasons that they do not belong to a group (e.g. "I wasn't invited", "they only laugh at the jokes of other people") than the reasons they do belong. School psychologists working with young people who do not feel like they belong challenge them to flip their thinking and look instead for all the evidence for why they *do* belong, why they *are* included and what is working *well*.

EVERYONE IS INTERESTED IN BELONGING

While many people may not actively focus on the issue of belonging, the subject has become a common interest across a wide variety of fields, including urban planning, architecture, art, design, media, medicine, engineering, economics and education. The broad acceptance of the importance of belonging seems to have stemmed from a growing recognition that it plays a vital role in our healthy functioning as people who are in a society. In 2009, the Centers for Disease Control and Prevention (CDC) in the United States prioritised belonging in their recommendations and strategies for schools. Increasing a sense of belonging was seen by the CDC as a matter of disease prevention, and Chapters 2 and 3 will examine the psychological and physical benefits that can flow from feeling that you belong across the lifespan.

EVOLUTIONARY PERSPECTIVES

Like many psychological constructs, we can trace our need to belong back to our prehistoric ancestors, for whom group life and cooperation were essential contributing factors to their safety and survival. Evolutionary theorists posit that a sense of belonging served as a survival mechanism for our ancient ancestors and that this drive and need for belonging remains an artefact from an earlier phase of evolution.

In the early stages of human history, people lived in small groups in which jobs like hunting, gathering and *sentinel* labour were shared. A person who lived a solitary life during these times faced enormous extra challenges to survive, and rejection from a group could thus have tragic consequences for an individual. These deep prehistoric roots offer one explanation as to why the fear of rejection persists today. Have you ever found yourself in conflict with someone else over a difference of opinion only to find yourself softening your stance or ending up in agreement? This tendency to soften positions to avoid social conflict is a part of the wider complex of tendencies that incline us to conform to social norms. A need to belong to others has been observed at both biological and neurological levels, providing compelling support for the claim that a desire for meaningful social relations is deeply embedded in our DNA. It seems plausible that a need to belong might still be underpinned by a genetic influence today. The increasing economic wealth of our society means that we can afford to live on our own and migrate away from the neighbourhoods in which we grew up. This is a supposed luxury that our ancient ancestors did not have, when living or even sleeping alone may not have been an option. While the modern-day solitary person is unlikely to fall prey to a deadly predator, we are still learning what kind of impact new social structures and living arrangements have on our psychological health.

WHAT CAN ANIMALS TEACH US ABOUT BELONGING?

The human ability to cooperate in a group, work together and seek benefits from belonging to others has much in common with the behaviour of other species. The ape family provides the most obvious point of comparison, but humans also share behavioural traits with animals as diverse as honeybees and ants, who also work together to build complex functioning societies (Tomasello, 2014).

The functions served by belonging in groups, or rather by collective group behaviour, differ significantly between species, but for many animals, the primary goals are predator avoidance, hunting, foraging and learning/teaching. In many species, young animals learn how to behave effectively by imitating older animals, in much the same way as many skills are passed on among humans. The ways that older humans connect and relate to others is observed by children, and through this social transmission of information, we learn valuable skills for interacting with others.

Several animal species have been shown to exhibit signs of empathy and compassion. This is particularly evident in service animals, whose connection to their owners is so powerful that they can sense their owners' triggers and signs of distress even before an incident occurs (Grove & Henderson, 2018). Animals in many species are also able to put the needs of others before their own. In one study, rhesus monkeys opted to starve to death rather than continue to pull a chain for food when pulling the chain also triggered pain in another monkey (Masserman, 1964).

We also know that some species feel social pain and may even mourn the loss of those to whom they are close. These behaviours are reflected in common stories about dogs waiting by the side of their deceased owner or the mournful sounds made by cows when their calves are removed. Animals belonging to certain species clearly have a deep sense of connection to others; when that connection is broken, it can cause great pain, just as is the case in humans.

The intimate relationships formed by animals can also shed light on the instinctive need to belong. Several species of animals mate for life, and most birds will choose another partner only once their current mate has died. Some species of bees like to sleep together and hold each other's feet while doing so. It is also worth considering the inbuilt homing instinct that many animals possess. Pigeons, turtles and salmon, for instance, are all able to travel long distances to migrate or to return home. This desire to move to shared destinations raises the question of whether it is connected to an intergenerational yearning to belong.

PHILOSOPHICAL ROOTS

Our modern Western understanding of belonging reflects and builds on the ideas of major early Greek and Roman thinkers. In Plato's Lysis, he depicts Socrates as being intimately concerned with the nature of friendship, and in Symposium, Plato has the comic playwright Aristophanes tell a story about the human soul's need for company and its constant quest to be reunited with its missing "other half". Aristotle later developed an influential categorisation of types of friendships in his Nichomachean Ethics, and the Stoics and Epicureans each made the place of the individual in society central to their views of the good life, albeit in different ways.

The Stoics developed an ethical theory called oikeiosis, which is close in Greek to belonging (from oikos, or household), though sometimes translated as appropriation. They argued that humans were naturally disposed to appropriate themselves to their environment and to the social groupings around them. One Stoic, Hierocles, in explaining the process of ethical development in the 2nd century CE, talks about thinking of concentric rings around a central point. The point is the individual and the rings are increasingly distant social relations – the closest ring is immediate family, then extended family, then the village, then the people in the broader region and on

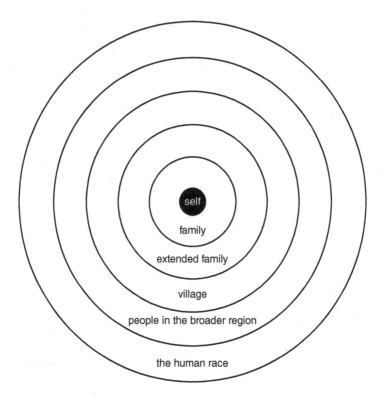

Figure 1.1 Adaption of Hierocles's model of concern.

outwards to the whole human race (Figure 1.1). The goal for the Stoic is to incrementally bring these concentric rings step by step into the centre, "appropriating" others to ourselves in such a way that we first treat our family as we would ourselves, our extended family as our family and so on. The goal is to appropriate the whole of humanity to ourselves by bringing the outer circle into the centre.

THEORIES OF BELONGING

According to Maslow's (1968, 1971) *Hierarchy of Needs*, the need for love and belongingness emerge once physiological and safety needs are satisfied, suggesting that they are fundamental for humans. Maslow holds that a failure to satisfy the need for belonging results in maladjustment and emotional distress, forcing people to invest their energies in meeting this deficit rather than in higher-level thought processes. Baumeister and Leary's (1995) seminal paper *The Need to Belong: Desire for Interpersonal Attachments as a Fundamental Human Motivation* also explores belongingness as a need, stating that human beings have an innate psychological drive to belong to groups and take part in meaningful social interactions. They state that "belongingness can be almost as compelling a need as food" (1995, pp. 497–529). The food metaphor is also deployed in Glasser's work (1986): "Hungry students think of food, lonely students look for friends" (p. 20). Most of us have experienced feeling starving only to open the fridge to see nothing appealing there at all. A common response to this situation is to eat something you take no pleasure in, but only for keeping those pangs of hunger at bay. Belonging can be a bit like this as well. As we will see in Chapter 6, a person's need to belong can be so compelling that if they cannot find a socially acceptable place to belong, they will seek to belong somewhere that is not socially accepted instead; a phenomenon that sheds light on the enduring appeal of gangs, cults and radicalised groups. Another less-extreme way that people often compensate for a lack of belonging is by investing deeply in one area of their life, to the detriment of other areas. For instance, if someone's sense of belonging to their family weakens over the years, they may go to great lengths to invest time and effort into their work, to strengthen their social relationships with their colleagues in order to fill the gap.

Although these theories concur in many respects on the status of belonging as a basic human need, they are concerned primarily with individuals and the pursuit of the individual need to belong. Although this certainly forms part of the bigger framework of issues connected to belonging, an individual-focused approach to the topic in some ways runs counter to the goal of increasing belonging at a societal level. In the widely quoted words of the late Chris Peterson, "other people matter" (Peterson, 2006, p. 249). Indeed, Peterson suggests that we can experience something in the company of others that he describes as *pure pleasure*. In fact, *sociometer theory* (Leary, 2010; Leary et al., 1995) states that all people possess a *sociometer*, an internal psychological system that monitors negative or positive social cues. Changes to a person's self-esteem because of these cues allow people to monitor whether there is a threat of rejection, which may influence their motivation towards engaging in behaviours that increase their social acceptance. While the sociometer is described as an internal gauge, core to this theory are the interactions with others within a social environment.

Few theories acknowledge that most people in society are intrinsically intertwined with complex systems and group processes, simply through their daily interactions. Systems theory (Von Bertalanffy, 1968) offers another perspective to help us grasp just how deeply embedded we are in our social contexts. Bronfenbrenner's ecological systems theory (1979), for example, offers a genuinely helpful way of examining belonging. Socioecological theories are concerned with the systems found in societies and suggest that, for most people, the family is the first unit to which a person belongs, followed by their school and local community, with each person belonging to an increasingly broad network of groups and systems as their lives progress. According to Bronfenbrenner (1979), people are at the centre of "layers" in their environment, which can have a significant effect on their lives. Similar to the philosophy outlined by the Stoics, these layers are presented in concentric rings usually described as microsystems, mesosystems, exosystems and macrosystems. The microsystem is the immediate environment (e.g. home, school, work), while the mesosystem layer describes the interactions among and between the individual's microsystems and broader systems. For example, for a child who is at the centre of the system, how their parents engage with their school teachers, peers and the parents of their peers are described in terms of the mesosystem. The layer described as the exosystem covers the broader settings that lie outside the immediate sphere of the individual, such as a local neighbourhood or community. Finally, the macrosystem includes the largest and most distant systems that are still present and influential on the life of an individual, such as their culture, values and political and economic systems. Research has found that all of the elements in the system interact with how a person belongs – from their culture, through their family, to something so impersonal as legislation (see Chapter 4, where the use of not belonging as a form of punishment is discussed) (Allen et al., 2016, 2018a, 2018b). Because of this, ecological systems provide a comprehensive means by which to investigate belonging in society. Imagine if your goal was to create a comprehensive solution to address loneliness in society by helping people who do not feel that they belong. You would not simply find the people in question more friends. Rather, you would need to look at the broader picture, at their neighbours, their community and the culture in which they are positioned. You would also need to ask how other systems help or hinder belonging and need to pay attention to the characteristics that individuals might have. The optimal routes to a solution might differ depending on whether a person values belonging, whether they have the skills to belong and whether they want to belong (see Chapter 7).

Bowlby (1988) offers another strong voice directed towards the examination of belonging. Bowlby's theory of attachment emphasises the importance of interactions between parents and their children in the early and formative years, stressing that these interactions inform the nature and quality of their future relationships. Attachment theory shows how pivotal these early bonds and relationships are in laying the groundwork for trust and relationships with other people throughout our lives. Bowlby's still face experiment is one of the most difficult experiments to observe as a parent. This approach studied the reactions of infants to a non-expressive (blank-faced) mother across three minutes of interaction. After the infants make repeated failed attempts to coax out of their mothers an expression or interaction, we see that the infants tended to withdraw and turn away from their mothers. The reaction, which may seem unsurprising, provides a glimmer of insight into how difficult early attachment may be for babies with parents dealing with mental health concerns (e.g. post-natal depression), substance use issues or who have attachment issues themselves.

One infamous experiment to test a child's attachment to their mother is Mary Ainsworth's strange situation classification (SSC). This original study, which has since been replicated many times, initially observed one hundred American infants aged between 12 and 18 months. The infants were observed through a two-way mirror to see how they responded when their mother left them with a stranger for a time before returning. Ainsworth and Bell (1970) identified three main attachment styles – secure, avoidant and resistant – and concluded that these attachment styles were formed because of early interactions with the mother. A child with a secure attachment would be distressed when their mother left, whereas an avoidant child would show no signs of distress. The behaviour of the child, when reunited with their mother, was also observed. Upon the mother's return, a securely attached child would typically be happy, whereas children with resistant or avoidant attachment would push the mother away or show little or no interest in their return. Ainsworth's work showed that there are many shades of attachment.

More recent research on maternal sensitivity has found that for children around six months of age, the mother's reaction during times of stress predicted a child's level of attachment security (Leerkes, 2011). These results emphasise the importance of being responsive, attentive, sensitive and empathetic in the earliest months of a child's life. An individual's sense of belonging is shaped by their early experiences (as we will see in more detail in Chapter 2), and this means that it is paramount that parents have the skills and abilities to facilitate healthy attachment from the beginning of their relationship with their child. When this is not the case, appropriate support needs to be made available to assist parent and child.

MEASURING BELONGING

The sense of belonging instrument (SOBI) is one of the most widely used measures of belonging currently available. This 27-item self-report measure, developed by Hagerty and Patusky (1995), consists of two distinct scales: the SOBI-P (psychological state), which measures sense of belonging in terms of valued involvement and fit in relationships, and the SOBI-A (antecedents), which examines events that happened in the past. The version of the SOBI provided next has been adapted slightly to make it a little more user-friendly (specifically item 4 of the SOBI-P has been adjusted).

SENSE OF BELONGING INSTRUMENT

Look at the statements in the following scales and rate them using the four-point Likert scale (1 = strongly agree, 2 = agree, 3 = disagree, 4 = strongly disagree) for the Sense of Belonging Psychological (SOBI-P) and (4 = strongly agree, 3 = agree, 2 = disagree, 1 = strongly disagree) for the Sense of Belonging Antecedents (SOBI-A). Think about the degree to which you experience a sense of belonging in a group, organisation or another environment. The total belonging score is a sum of the scores of the individual items and can range from 27 to 108, with higher scores indicating a greater sense of belonging.

Sense of Belonging Psychological (SOBI-P)

Items	Strongly agree (1)	Agree (2)	Disagree (3)	Strongly disagree (4)
1 I often wonder if there is any place on earth where I really fit in.				
2 I am just not sure if I fit in with my friends.				
3 I would describe myself as a misfit in most social situations.				
4 I generally feel that people do not accept me.				
5 I feel like a piece of a jig-saw puzzle that doesn't fit into the puzzle.				

Items	Strongly agree (1)	Agree (2)	Disagree (3)	Strongly disagree (4)
6 I would like to make a difference to people or things around me, but I don't feel what I have to offer is valued.				
7 I feel like an outsider in most situations.				
8 I am troubled by feeling like I have no place in this world.				
9 I could disappear for days and it wouldn't matter to my family.				
10 In general, I don't feel a part of the mainstream of society.				
11 I feel like I observe life rather participate in it.				
12 If I died tomorrow, very few people would come to my funeral.				
13 I feel like a square peg trying to fit into a round hole.				
14 I don't feel that there is any place where I really fit in this world.				
15 I am uncomfortable that my background and experiences are so different from those who are usually around me.				
16 I could not see or call my friends for days and it wouldn't matter to them.				

Items	Strongly agree (1)	Agree (2)	Disagree (3)	Strongly disagree (4)
17 I feel left out of things.				
18 I am not valued by or important to my friends.				
				SCORE

Sense of Belonging Antecedents (SOBI-A)

Items	Strongly agree (4)	Agree (3)	Disagree (2)	Strongly disagree (1)
19 It is important to me that I am valued or accepted by others.				
20 In the past, I have felt valued and important to others.				
21 It is important to me that I fit somewhere in this world.				
22 I have qualities that can be important to others.				
23 I am working on fitting in better with those around me.				
24 I want to be a part of things going on around me.				
25 It is important to me that my thoughts and opinions are valued.				
26 Generally, other people recognize my strengths and good points.				
27 I can make myself fit in anywhere.				
				SCORE
		TOTAL SCORE (Add SOBI-P + SOBI-A)		

Source: Reprinted with permission from B. Hagerty (Hagerty & Patusky, 1995)

Was your score higher or lower than you might have anticipated? The SOBI shows a strong relationship with measures of depression and loneliness. If your score was low, and you are feeling unsatisfied with your level of belonging, please reach out to your support networks, including your GP or local helplines for further support, and perhaps also to discuss how you may be able to feel more satisfied with your sense of belonging.

2

BELONGING BEGINS
AT BIRTH

Belonging is often said to begin at birth. Despite the absence of research in this area, it is reasonable to suppose that the conditions underlying how a person feels belonging begin to be set in place even before conception. Any parent who has experienced the physical loss of a baby during pregnancy or the conceptual loss of a baby when finding out that they cannot conceive knows the pain associated with the loss of the potential future bond with a child. It is widely accepted that the innate motivation we have to connect with others is deeply embedded in our biological makeup. The aim of this chapter is to demonstrate the fundamental importance of belonging, from the earliest stages of our lives and even back to the formative periods that precede them. We will consider the biological studies and neuropsychological research that have emphasised the importance of belonging for individuals in their early years through to adolescence.

BELONGING IS IN OUR BIOLOGY

From the moment we are born, we strive to connect to our primary caregivers. Of course, this makes sense biologically. Our primary caregivers are the same people who ensure our wellbeing and provide food, safety and shelter. If we were somehow capable of rejecting our caregivers from birth, we would find ourselves in all sorts of trouble. Compared to other mammals, baby humans are one of the most helpless species. Most mammals can learn to walk shortly after birth; others can swim; and some birds are born with a full set of flight feathers. A six-month-old panda can climb a tree, whereas a baby human of the same age is barely capable of sitting independently. The reason for this comparative helplessness is a biological trade-off that sacrifices the independence of human newborns to ensure they are small enough to pass safely from their mothers' bodies into the waiting world. Due to their helplessness, humans have no choice but to belong to their parents or other caregivers from birth. Indeed, that we do so is, in fact, critical to our survival.

Neuroscientist Mathew Lieberman suggests in his book *Social* that we never actually switch off our thoughts about others and our relationships to them (Lieberman, 2013). Put simply, our brain enters a "default network" state when resting which mirrors the neural activity that occurs when we engage in social interaction. Lieberman suggests that when we shut our eyes and attempt to clear our minds, most of us will innately think of others or of ourselves in relation to others. Why don't you try it right now? Close your eyes, try to clear your mind and see what thoughts arise. The default network has been observed in babies as young as two weeks old, providing evidence that we are indeed born to belong.

BELONGING FOR BABIES, CHILDREN AND ADOLESCENTS

We can now turn to consider how crucial belonging is to us from the day we are born and how it informs every developmental milestone and stage in our lives.

INFANCY

Immediately after birth, when a baby is first placed on its mother's abdomen, it will, in most cases, find its way instinctively to the breast to feed. The *breast crawl* serves a dual benefit to both mother and baby in terms of bonding. Extended contact after birth has been found to be associated with a range of benefits, including decreased risk of failure to thrive and even decreased risk of child abuse and parental neglect later. In some small way, the clumsy, haphazard, yet intentional crawl from abdomen to breast symbolises the early phases of belonging for infants by manifesting their connection to one of the most important relationships they will have in their lives.

The need to belong is present from the moment of birth, and the skills associated with belonging emerge early on in life as well (Over, 2016). From around six to eight weeks, most babies will begin to exhibit social behaviour. Babies can be observed smiling at caregivers as early as six weeks, and by 12 weeks can be seen smiling at others. Verbal exchanges between infant and caregivers also begin to emerge around this time. These are verbal exchanges with reciprocal turn-taking, something like conversational ping-pong but with babble instead of fully formed words. We can also see joint attention develop during this period, with the young baby showing a desire to give their attention to objects and interesting stimuli. The ability to imitate emerges from these early stages, and this skill plays an important role in the transmission of social information. Think back to the Bowlby's still face experiment discussed in Chapter 1. Imagine how detrimental to these processes non-responsiveness at these early stages of development would be.

Around the 14–18-month mark, babies go through a phase – which many parents will remember with great frustration – in which they learn to throw their dummy, teddy or other objects to the ground. If the object is returned to them, it will promptly be thrown down again and again. As tedious as this game may become for the caregiver, it marks an important development in our social growth and an early indication of our natural and innate desire to connect with one another. A game that seems to involve the rejection of an item is actually a game that facilitates bonding.

The most compelling evidence of our need to belong from birth can be found in the consequences of the absence of belonging. In cases of abuse, neglect or disorganised attachment, the absence of a sense of belonging has a devastating impact on psychological and social functioning, which extends through childhood and adolescence and well into adulthood. There are many examples in the social psychological literature of the effects of social isolation at a young age (Braddock & Gonzalez, 2010; Matthews et al., 2016). A famous case discussed in many undergraduate psychology classes as an example of the effects of isolation and neglect is that of Genie Wiley.

Genie (a pseudonym) suffered complex trauma during childhood (Fromkin et al., 1974). From infancy, her father would strap her to a toilet and force her to wear a straitjacket that restricted arm movements for up to 13 hours a day. She was physically abused with a bat and prohibited from talking or crying. Genie developed several physiological problems and developmental delays such as the inability to chew, swallow, walk or focus her eyes. Children in such situations are often referred to rather cruelly as feral, but the reality is that these outcomes are, for the most part, the consequence of significant abuse and neglect on the part of adults (Fromkin et al., 1974).

When belonging is interrupted, particularly in extreme cases like Genie's, the children involved do not have the opportunity to learn human social behaviours from peers or adults, and their language development may also be delayed. Their future relationships are impeded, and the devastating consequences of their abuse are often lifelong.

The human connections that are so fundamental at birth and in the first months and years of life are equally relevant at each later stage and especially as we enter older age.

EARLY CHILDHOOD

Early childhood is a developmental period marked by significant physical and cognitive growth. When we think about child development and school readiness at this stage, we often think about academic-orientated gains and maybe a few motor skills: Do they know their colours? Can they count to ten? Can they read their own name? Can they dress themselves? Can they open a lunch box? However, the social development that occurs in this period is just as crucial for school readiness. Sharing, turn-taking, regulating emotions, making decisions about play and resolving conflict are among the skills that begin to emerge at this age but which may take years to consolidate. In early childhood, we begin to see children engage in behaviour that increases social interaction and demonstrates the development of social behaviour and even moral development. We see children move into a phase in which friendships are formed, a phase in which they no longer just play alongside their peers but play with their peers.

Young children at this age seek social acceptance from peers and adults and in doing so begin to demonstrate social conformity. In a 2011 study, Haun and Tomasello administered a modified Asch Task to a group of four-year-olds. The children were divided into groups of four, three of whom were given the same (correct) picture to look at while one child was given a different (incorrect) picture. All the children were asked a question that related to the visual stimulus given to the three children with the correct picture, creating a situation in which the child who was given something else would be unable to answer accurately. The results of the experiment were interesting: when the children with the images that corresponded to the question were asked the question first, the child with the alternative picture would respond in the same way – even though their picture did not match the question. This provides strong evidence for the supposition that behaviour related to social conformity begins early in life. Children seek social acceptance from others to such a strong degree that they are willing to share incorrect answers to avoid the risk of being part of an outgroup.

In adults, phenomena that take similar forms to the behaviour found in this experiment are often referred to as "groupthink" (a term borrowed by psychologists from George Orwell's 1984). Groupthink takes place when the desire for social conformity takes place at the expense of rational decision-making. Individuals avoid voicing opinions or reporting facts that depart from the collective beliefs of the group in order to avoid conflict. The result can be the creation of an environment in which only collective agreement is socially acceptable. The group can become resistant to new evidence, which can lead to poor decision-making and a lack of critical evaluation. This phenomenon shows just how much value humans place on belonging to a group: at times they are willing to censor their own speech and even their thoughts to retain group membership and approval.

Young children are strongly aware of inclusive and exclusive types of play behaviour from an early age. Belonging is closely linked to inclusion and peer acceptance, with group approval as the cornerstone of a sense of belonging to a peer group at this stage. As we will see in Chapter 4, children can find themselves ostracised from peer groups because their behaviour or physical attributes diverge from group norms. It is therefore vital that young children learn inclusive behaviours and hear messages advocating tolerance and acceptance. Social skills are also important at this age. Many children in this age group go through a phase of testing boundaries – testing the limits of rules at home and school while testing limits with peers as well. It is not uncommon for children of this age who lack interactive social skills or vocabulary to engage in behaviour that is not appropriate (e.g. pushing others). These children may have a strong desire to interact with others without yet having the skills to play in an appropriate way. It is crucial, then, that these children are not simply delivered a consequence for their behaviour but are also taught the necessary skills to interact appropriately.

CHILDHOOD

Relationships outside of the home increase during childhood, and school becomes an important locus of belonging for most children, especially with regard to student–teacher relationships. Most children endeavour to conform to social norms most of the time. This is because children become more conscious about matching their behaviour to that of their peers, marking an important point in the development of their need to belong and feel included.

An understanding of the thoughts, feelings and intentions of others can be detected in children as young as five years old. Some researchers describe this development as the child forming an emerging theory of mind. A famous test for theory of mind is the Sally-Anne test created by Simon Baron-Cohen and colleagues (1985). This involves showing a child a cartoon with two characters: Sally and Anne. In the cartoon, Sally has a basket and Anne has a box. Sally also has a marble. She puts the marble into her basket then leaves the room to go for a walk. While Sally is away, Anne takes the marble from the basket and places it in her box. The child is then asked where Sally should look for her marble upon her return. A child who is able to predict the intentions of others will say that Sally will look in her basket for the marble. The acquisition of theory of mind is understood to be a developmental process, one that fits around the concept of empathy. Empathy facilitates a sense of belongingness through our ability to put ourselves in someone else's shoes. Research suggests that empathy is a distinct psychological construct in predicting children's social functioning (Wang & Wang, 2015).

Studies have also found that children display a strong desire to be viewed positively, to form social bonds and to manage a reputation. Important support for this comes from work on reputation management that shows that young children are less likely to engage in antisocial behaviours such as stealing when they are being watched by a peer or adult (compared to when they are on their own; Engelmann et al., 2012). This shows that the children are beginning to understand the importance of peer approval and inclusion at school and are less willing to act in ways that risk losing approval and inclusion, regardless of their views about any underlying moral status of their actions. Sadly, patterns of social rejection in the schoolyard can become entrenched in play behaviours. Negative reputations can develop, leading to children being labelled as problematic, thus cementing the perceptions of others in a way that leads to a feedback loop of further exclusion.

Those children who lack the foundations needed to belong in childhood report increased levels of dysfunction, psychosocial disturbance and difficulties later in life. Messages directed at building positive relationships and belonging in childhood – from both parents and particularly schools – are therefore fundamental tools for helping to build strong foundations for empathy, acceptance and tolerance of others as a child grows.

ADOLESCENCE

While a sense of belonging is important for children, we know that belonging is especially important for adolescents. Adolescence is sometimes described as the period during which young people rely less on their parents for social support. This is certainly the case for younger teenagers: peer groups and the need to belong become more important for social identity, psychosocial adjustment, coping, resiliency, and ultimately, the transition into adulthood. Younger adolescents have been found to draw advice and social support from their peers more so than older adolescents.

Self-presentation and reputation management become central concerns for adolescents as they learn social norms and boundaries. Children and adolescents with poor or limited social and emotional competencies, such as emotional regulation, can encounter issues related to belonging. Consequently, a solid understanding of social skills and successful social development is a foundation for belonging at this age.

Researchers have often wondered whether the need to belong changes across the lifespan of the individual, and it is thanks to research focused on adolescence that we can now begin to understand how detrimental "not belonging" can be for this age group. Adolescents appear to be more sensitive to ostracism than any other age group. One explanation for this may be related to the neural development that occurs during this period. Adolescence is marked by complex processes of neural attrition and growth. Neural imaging research shows that during adolescence, the brain undergoes a unique trajectory of neural development and maturation in regions that are involved in the processing of complex social interactions and frameworks (Arain et al., 2013; Burnett et al., 2011). Adolescence is also marked by the development of social identity, to which a sense of belonging is critical (Friedman, 2007). Social identity is defined as a person's sense of *who they are* and it is informed by their membership to groups. The different groups (e.g. family, friends, clubs, hobbies) to which people belong contribute to how people perceive themselves (Tajfel & Turner, 1979). Finding a group in which a person can really be themselves and at the same time feel safe, respected, cared for and liked is important for many people's sense of belonging. For adolescents, this acceptance might be found in a family group, but it is more common for adolescents to look to a peer group or school group as they seek to extend their social identity beyond the family unit. As peer groups become increasingly important, social isolation and exclusion equally have an increasingly direct negative effect on psychosocial adjustment and transition into adulthood.

Beverly Daniel Tatum asks in her book *Why Are All the Black Kids Sitting Together in the Cafeteria?* what is often a burning question for staff working in secondary schools and frequently also for students themselves as well. Tatum notes that the title question in itself is revealing, since nobody asks why all the white students sit together; even the framing of the issue identifies a primary group and a group marked by difference. In early childhood, it is typical to see young children of different races mixing together, but during adolescence, we see the separation of ethnic and cultural groups of all types, a phenomenon that is not specific to Black adolescents. It is easy to see why Tatum believes that so-called self-segregation is a developmental process that has its origins in a response to the environmental stressor of racism and that adolescents as a coping strategy join cultural groups with which they identify.

We know that Black history is steeped in racism and messages of exclusion in many parts of the Western world. These messages are amplified for adolescents in educational settings, with their particular sensitivity to the undercurrents at play in ingroup membership (Gray et al., 2018).

> Scholars acknowledge that race and identity are critical for understanding patterns of belonging, motivation, and performance because stigmatized social identity groups such as Black Americans are at a heightened risk of receiving disconfirming messages about whether they fit within academic spaces.
>
> (Gray et al., 2018, p. 1)

They further ask,

> What opportunities do Black students have to establish a sense of belonging when school systems have historically prohibited Black people from receiving formal education and are currently complicit in inequitable education?
>
> (Gray et al., 2018, p. 1)

Both Tatum and Gray acknowledge as problematic the fact that the identity development of Black teenagers, and teenagers of other racial minority groups elsewhere around the world, can often have consequences that increase future cycles of exclusion due to cultural stereotypes and ingroup norms that devalue academic achievement. While stereotypes and heuristics are a normal cognitive process, they can exaggerate differences and similarities between people and perpetuate bias. Examining race in this way is deeply complex, especially when othering can occur within the same race, such as in the case of different skin tones (Sapolsky, 2017). Gray and colleagues (2018) present the example of clothing emblazoned with explicit or implicit phraseology or symbols intended to convey race-related identity beliefs. In some cases, these may aim to promote or deter connections to other spheres of belonging, such as school and achievement. However, as Gray and colleagues point out, a "colour-blind" approach to managing race-related issues can be problematic because issues of prejudice and discrimination can be ignored altogether.

As this example shows, belonging is not an unmitigated good and can be paradoxical in many ways. Belonging to an outgroup means not belonging to an ingroup, and exclusion from an outgroup can lead some to look towards other means of belonging and spaces where they can feel accepted. This might lead some to seek alignment with mainstream societal norms, whereas others may be pushed towards the extremes in their search for acceptance and belonging.

Identity formation is a key feature of adolescent development. During this time, adolescents develop emotional maturity needed to make choices regarding future directions in adulthood. Belonging is also important for psychosocial adjustment. Priorities and expectations with respect to belonging change as the individual transitions from childhood to adolescence. For example, in preadolescence and early adolescence, friendship groups and a sense of belonging play a pivotal role in the transition to high school. During adolescence, belonging to groups takes on an increasing importance for the individual, and group membership plays an important role in the shaping of social identity. Thus, friendships play a key role in providing social identity as well as social support, both of which are mechanisms for supporting psychosocial adjustment and wellbeing during adolescence (Mensah et al., 2013).

A sense of belonging to friendship groups has been found to ease the sometimes rocky and tumultuous transition into adulthood (Quinn & Oldmeadow, 2013). It can be particularly important during middle adolescence, when friendship changes occur and feelings of disconnection towards school can be felt. Negative experiences related to a sense of belonging during adolescence can have a profoundly negative impact on psychosocial adjustment (Allen et al., 2014). Involvement in extracurricular activities may assist in buffering these negative effects, offering youth with new groups to which they can belong, but research points to a decline in youth participation in ingroups outside of school. There are fewer young people engaged in team sports and in regular outside play than there was in previous generations (The Aspen Institute, 2019).

BELONGING TO SCHOOL

Schools offer important opportunities for children and adolescents to belong. This sense of belonging can transcend generations and can last well beyond the time that the individual leaves school and ventures out into the wider world. Parents with adult children may speak fondly about the school they attended themselves or even reminisce about their own involvement in the school that their children attended. For many children and young people, schools can offer a central and communal experience of belonging. School belonging has been found to be positively associated with academic motivation, wellbeing, self-concept and self-esteem. It is known to reduce the likelihood of truancy, school dropout and substance use and to buffer the effects of suicidal ideation, depression and anxiety (Abdollahi et al., 2020; Arslan et al., 2020; McMahon et al., 2004; Pittman & Richmond, 2007; Shochet et al., 2006; Wyman et al., 2019).

Feelings of affiliation and attachment can vary in type and degree among students. A high sense of school belonging correlates with positive psychological functioning at school, such as self-esteem, ability to cope with problems as they arise, improved mental health and academic motivation (Allen & Boyle, 2016; Slaten et al., 2016). School belonging is inversely related to school dropout rates, truancy and risk-taking behaviours. It is no surprise that students are more likely to enjoy and be interested in school and classwork when they feel a positive sense of belonging to peers and teachers. A higher sense of belonging also positively correlates with students' "commitment to their work, higher expectations of success, and lower levels of anxiety" (Osterman, 2000, p. 331).

When students do not feel a sense of belonging to school, they may act in ways that challenge the other factors that influence their sense of belonging (e.g. positive relationships with others) and seek belonging elsewhere (Okonofua et al., 2016). Students are less likely to turn to deviant peers for a sense of belonging if they have formed meaningful and positive relationships with fellow classmates and teachers (Lenzi et al., 2019). Disturbingly, recent research has shown that a low sense of attachment to school is a common connecting factor linking school shootings, suicidal behaviour in adolescence and youth radicalisation.

In nearly all school shootings that have been studied, the perpetrators appear to have felt little attachment to their schools, teachers and peers. The research carried out by Wike and Fraser (2009) found concerning evidence that shootings occur in schools that have higher degrees of social stratification, strained relationships between teachers and students and fewer opportunities for school-sanctioned activities. In this research, schools that were at greatest risk of gun violence did not provide individualised support to students and had school climates characterised by disrespectful behaviour towards peers and teachers and by bullying (Roffey & Boyle, 2018).

According to Professor John Hattie (2002), 95% of five-year-olds want to come to school to learn, a figure that drops to 30% by the end of primary school and then rises slightly in high school. For most, then, it seems that school – as a learning institution – is not an inviting place to belong. A cross-national survey of data from 72 countries suggests that as many as one in three students does not feel a sense of belonging to their school. Worryingly, the proportion of students who do not feel like they belong has grown over the past decade, but this issue has so far received little in the way of a concerted response from policymakers and governments (Allen et al., 2019; Roffey et al., 2019).

STUDENT-TEACHER RELATIONSHIP

My own research has found that of all the predictors associated with a sense of belonging to school, the strength of student–teacher relationships was the most powerful (Allen et al., 2018). Yet how we nurture that relationship in a climate of high teacher stress, standardised testing, high attrition rates among graduate teachers and high levels of teacher burnout raises more than a few questions (Allen & Kern, 2017, 2019). An analysis of 27,500 teachers in the UK who trained between 2011 and 2015 found that one-quarter of those who graduated had left the profession within three years. Data from Australia captured through the Hunter Institute of Mental Health found that up to half of the 453 Australian teachers sampled left the profession in the first five years after graduation. Those questioned in the study cited not having enough time and having too much work as the biggest challenge of the job. It seems possible, then, that teachers do not have either the time or the resources to build the important connections they need with their students.

One thing we do know is that the strength of teachers' sense of belonging to their schools predicts their students' sense of belonging. Teacher welfare thus needs to be urgently evaluated as part of any strategy for increasing school belonging among students. However, mandatory programmes or professional development may run counter to what well-meaning leadership is trying to achieve. Likewise, introducing additional burdens and pressure by asking teachers to run interventions and produce dazzling new strategies to increase student belonging may also be at odds with building belonging in school communities. A better approach may be to provide teachers with more time and resources and to ask them directly what would strengthen their own sense of belonging.

We also know that a teacher's sense of belonging to the school principal's ingroup can also help mitigate many of the challenges that teachers experience and increase psychological safety (Gerlach & Gockel, 2018). Finding ways to strengthen the teacher-principal relationship thus also seems likely to have significant effects on student and staff belonging to school.

NEGATIVE STUDENT–TEACHER RELATIONSHIPS

Significant research describes the importance of the student–teacher relationship in fostering a sense of school belonging. Unfortunately, not all students experience their relationships with their teachers as supportive, and some instead find that they are labelled as falling into a problematic group at an early point in their school career. Some teachers treat students differently based on their race, gender, appearance, ability, socioeconomic status and more. This type of differential treatment can significantly decrease a student's chances of success (Osterman, 2000). Negative school experiences can create a weak connection to teachers and the school community, leading to disengagement from the classroom and peers (Wallace et al., 2012) and may ultimately result in school dropout. Studies examining students who have dropped out from school show that feelings of alienation or ostracism from a school community, teachers or fellow students can be a primary driver for the decision to leave school early.

The Program for International Student Assessment (PISA) data also offers some clues concerning the social challenges facing young people:

> 35% of students reported that at least a few times per month their teachers called on them less than they called on others; 21% said their teachers gave them the impression they were less intelligent than they were; 18% of students reported that their teachers grade them more harshly than others; 14% reported that their teachers discipline them more harshly than others; 10% reported their teachers ridicule them; 9% reported their teachers insult them in front of others; boys were more likely than girls to report that their teachers did not treat them fairly.
>
> (OECD, 2017, p. 126)

HOW CAN WE CREATE SPHERES OF BELONGING FOR YOUNG PEOPLE?

Some of the most effective methods for fostering school belonging include the following:

(a) implementing high standards and expectations and providing academic support to all students; (b) applying fair and consistent disciplinary policies that are collectively agreed upon and fairly enforced; (c) creating trusting relationships among students,

teachers, staff, administrators, and families; (d) hiring and supporting capable teachers skilled in content, teaching techniques,
and classroom management to meet each leaner's needs; (e) fostering high parent/family expectations for school performance
and school completion; and (f) ensuring that every student feels
close to at least one supportive adult at school.

(Wingspread Declaration on School
Connections, 2004, p. 233)

Osterman (2000) asserts that it is the responsibility of teachers
and schools to encourage a sense of belonging and community in
the school, through the creation and implementation of communal
activities and learning opportunities. Specific training in collaborative
techniques among teachers and students has the potential to significantly increase the number of students who have a greater sense of
school belonging (Lenzi et al., 2019).

The goal of building belonging in schools should be integrated
with ongoing practices that already occur throughout a typical school
day rather than being added as an extra task. Professor Kathryn Riley
emphasised that schools cannot simply tell their students that they
need to belong because belonging is not a behaviour that can be
demanded or required. Rather, schools need to prioritise, value and
teach social and emotional competencies, which can help lay solid
foundations for a culture of belonging.

The need for early-years approaches is recognised in Australia
though The Early Years Framework's "Being, Becoming, and Belonging",
which prioritises the need to belong at a young age. In pursuing the
goals of this framework, it is necessary to strive to create a culture of
social inclusion so that acceptance, inclusion and empathy towards
others become social norms. The work of Vivian Paley and her rule
"You can't say you can't play" (YCSYCP) provide one approach to creating a norm around belonging for children as young as three years of
age. By the time children begin primary school, social rules around
exclusion and ostracisation are already entrenched. Consequently,

early intervention is critical to making a difference. YCSYCP sets the scene for inclusion and belonging as soon as children are old enough to understand it as a social rule.

Professor Amanda Harrist has built on Paley's social rule by developing an intervention around it (Harrist & Bradley, 2003). We learn from her research that the rule should be introduced early on, alongside other class rules, because patterns of rejection can become established quickly. Harrist also advises that there needs to be understanding and buy-in by the children, along with lots of roleplay, coaching and modelling. A randomised, controlled test of the intervention for children with obesity in 29 rural schools found that obese children in the YCSYCP classrooms had significantly lower weight over the following three years than children in the control group classrooms. These results convey important information, because obesity can be a sign of emotional distress and a source of rejection by peers.

Tackling social competence early on is also widely recommended in the scholarship on belonging. During the early years, skills that facilitate a sense of belonging include turn-taking, emotional regulation, coping skills, inclusive play behaviours, language and communication skills (Allen et al., 2017; St. Amand et al., 2017; Frydenberg et al., 2012). Proactively providing children with these skills can reduce exclusion and increase belonging by making it easier for children to know how to behave in a way that is conducive to group activity.

Professor Greg Walton's research on social belonging interventions has older students talk to younger students about the challenges they may have faced in belonging when they transitioned to high school or university. The younger students get to hear from older students representing various social and demographic groupings that they too were worried about their belonging when they first started and that they may also have experienced negative events that are just a normal part of the transition. Walton found that when students understand that the challenges of transition are common and improvable and that those early feelings of a lack of belonging are not permanent, they are able to infer that the same events happening to them need not mean that they do not belong. Instead, these events are recast as just a normative part of the transition. When students see challenges as normal difficulties that can be overcome, they stay more engaged in school.

WHY DO WE NEED TO PROMOTE POSITIVE INTERACTIONS IN SCHOOLS?

In addition to promoting belonging in schools because a sense of belonging meets a fundamental human need, fostering belonging also serves as a protective factor for those children who are most vulnerable. In almost all education systems worldwide, socioeconomically disadvantaged students and students from minority backgrounds

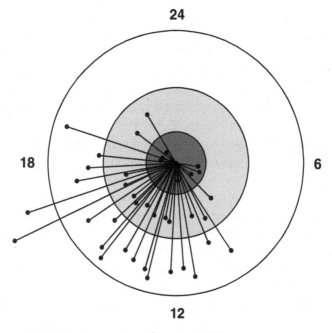

Figure 2.1 Positive interactions of a typical child.

Source: Adapted from Ludy-Dobson & Perry, 2010. Reprinted with permission from B. Perry

report a lower sense of belonging than do more advantaged students (Uwah et al., 2008). Addressing a sense of school belonging in these groups has been shown to close the achievement gap by as much as 50%–60% (Gehlbach et al., 2016; Walton, 2014).

Research from Christine Ludy-Dobson and Bruce Perry (2010) demonstrates that children with trauma histories can be vulnerable to low belonging due to the lack of positive interactions they may have over the course of a typical day. Figure 2.1 shows a 24-hour map over a two-week period. The arrows represent positive interactions. The arrows that can be seen in the inner circle represent positive interactions with family. The arrows in the next circle represent positive interactions with friends. Arrows that reach to the larger

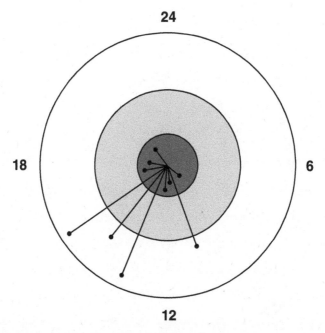

Figure 2.2 Positive interactions of a child in foster care.

Source: Adapted from Ludy-Dobson & Perry, 2010. Reprinted with permission from B. Perry

circle represent positive interactions with classmates/acquaintances. Arrows outside the circle represent interactions with strangers. Figure 2.1 represents a typical child, whereas Figure 2.2 represents a child in foster care. The stark contrast between the figures show how different people can experience social interactions and that those who need them the most may not be getting them.

Belonging in childhood and adolescence is fundamental to psychological wellbeing. As we will see in the Chapter 3, the benefits of belonging during the school years can have lasting effects well into adulthood.

3

BELONGING IN ADULTHOOD

Research has demonstrated that individuals who report a sense of belonging to groups and networks in childhood and adolescence are more likely to exhibit positive psychological functioning across a range of variables in adulthood. Moreover, having a sense of belonging in the adult years is also associated with a range of benefits, including physical health and longevity. Here we will discuss belonging as it relates to early adulthood and extends into the later years of our lives.

PUTTING THE "LONG" IN *BELONG*

The benefits associated with a sense of belonging to school appear to continue to pay off later in life as well. Young people with a sense of belonging at school also report a greater overall sense of psychological wellbeing in adulthood (O'Connor et al., 2010).

Steiner and colleagues examined the relationship between family and school belonging among adolescents and its health-related outcomes during adulthood. This longitudinal study involved the participation of 14,800 adolescents who had self-reported their risk behaviours and experiences through to adulthood. The effects of school connectedness as a protective factor in adulthood seemed to support the reduction of emotional distress, suicidal ideation, violence, victimisation, problematic sexual behaviours and drug use. And these effects continued to have enduring power over a decade into adult life. We can conclude from this that investing in belongingness in childhood and adolescence has long-term benefits that stretch far beyond the immediate application of the investment.

YOUNG ADULTHOOD

Erikson's (1950) psychosocial development theory suggests that the need for belonging felt by young adults is just as pressing as it is for adolescents. For young adults, finding a place to belong contributes to a meaningful life and is positively associated with self-efficacy, life satisfaction and, more generally, wellbeing (O'Connor et al., 2010; Haslam et al., 2009).

Emerging young adulthood is a critical developmental phase that is often neglected in the psychological literature. Members of this age group are expected to be more or less launched on their way through life when they leave adolescence, but neurological research makes clear that the brain continues to develop during this period; a process that can carry on until the age of 30 for men and the early to mid-20s for women. Many of the significant changes that occur upon entering adulthood take place at the societal, individual and biological level.

Throughout adulthood, societal changes heavily influence the way we form bonds and friendships with others. As a society, we are exposed to a constant stream of larger and smaller changes in the ways we live, work and care for our children. More mothers than ever before are working today, but there are still more stay-at-home mothers than stay-at-home fathers. For young mothers, the tug of war that can occur between work pressures and family demands can lead to the attrition of friendships as social interactions become deprioritised as luxuries in contrast to these other two "essential" domains.

Mobility can also present as a barrier for belonging in adulthood. Relocating for work is sometimes necessary, and transitioning between places may occur regularly. Belonging in the workplace can create an important sphere of belonging for many adults, especially through co-workers and colleagues. However, the disconnection that a person may feel from the place where they grew up, and from their family and the friends of their youth, can lead to feelings of not belonging and can cause problems when it comes to making new and meaningful connections. Challenges also arise for those who work remotely or from home, where the potential for connections with others is reduced or completely absent.

Other social changes may also provide challenges for belonging in adulthood. Up to 90% of adults introduce themselves to their neighbours, but only 50% know their name. Impromptu social visits are almost unheard of. It may be possible that adults today are not spending the same amount of time connecting with others compared to previous generations. Certainly, Putnam (2000) points to a decline in church membership and attendance. Church is no longer instrumental in providing a place of community togetherness in Western culture, whereas it was once. The increasing absence of church leaves many to wonder what has replaced it.

Despite the many challenges in maintaining social bonds, a sense of belonging during adulthood has been found to be an important supporting factor for both physical and mental health. Friendships among young adults may offer social support, which can be important for coping with negative life experiences and rapid social changes that occur in young adulthood (Barry et al., 2015). It may also be possible that a sense of belonging can help stave off loneliness experienced in this age group particularly for vulnerable populations (Allen, 2020).

MID ADULTHOOD

Middle age is a distinctive period after young adulthood and before the onset of old age. Erikson (1950) identified people between 40 and 65 years as in their middle adulthood phase. This period can be a time in which you re-examine your life by assessing achievements and accomplishments. There has been less research on belonging into mid-adulthood than on other age groups, but this period remains a critical time for belonging. In fact, life satisfaction in this stage is often evaluated more explicitly by reference to inner fulfilment and contentedness than it is in earlier periods. Transition into retirement or relocation can create a loss of relationships and can shift perceptions of social identity. Family structures and relationships that were previously perceived as secure can be challenged for members of this age group. For example, the relocation of members of the younger generation can result in less-mutual involvement with extended families and grandparents, causing a sense of loss or lack. Divorce and separation can also cause disruption in relationships in this age group. These threats to social connections may create the same neural and physiological response that occurs when people encounter other critical survival threats, such as the threat to personal safety or of physical harm. Such events can also lead to implications for physical and mental health.

Group life becomes increasingly important in middle adulthood, and research tells us that joining groups and finding a sense of belonging is a key element in improving our lives. However, concerningly, reports from the UK suggest that the number of people over 50 who experience loneliness will reach two million by 2026. We know that group life is linked to an increased lifespan and to improved resistance to infectious diseases. Research by Cruwys and colleagues (2013) found that for those age 50 and above with a history of depression, simply joining a social group could decrease their risk of relapse by 24% and joining three social groups could decrease their risk by 63%.

It is well established that sedentary behaviour is a crucial risk factor for poor physical health; however, it may also seem that there are implications for one's sense of belonging. One study investigated the link between community belonging and adult sedentary behaviour during leisure time. The researchers found that those in middle adulthood who were more active and less sedentary had a stronger sense of community belonging than those who displayed more sedentary behaviours (Anderson et al., 2016). It may be possible that a sense of community belonging is achieved through active participation in community programmes, events and activities rather than being sedentary or socially withdrawn. This is because community participation provides another avenue for creating a sense of belonging.

One risk factor for low belonging in adulthood is living alone. Several studies have suggested that living alone is a risk factor for depression when belongingness needs are not being satisfied (Kim et al., 2017). A recent study examined the relationship between living alone, a sense of belonging and depressive symptoms among Australian men in their late adulthood or those age 60 and above. The results of the study indicated that those who live alone have an increased risk of developing depressive symptoms due to low levels of a sense of belongingness or its complete absence (McLaren, 2020). This provides further evidence for the relevance and importance of a sense of belonging in each life stage.

OLDER AGE

Older age can also be a vulnerable time for belonging, especially when the need for belonging is not met (Theeke et al., 2015). Indeed, low belonging has been identified as a key risk factor for loneliness, and loneliness and social isolation are both linked to an increased risk of several mental and physical health problems. The Administration for Community Living's Administration on Aging (2018), under the US Department of Health and Human Services, reported that approximately 13 million older adults live alone. Physical and cognitive limitations can prevent and restrict social connections, with the evidence suggesting that many older adults in residential care do not feel a sense of belonging to their facility. A natural loss of friendships due to deaths in an ageing demographic can compound feelings of isolation that have a negative effect on lifespan and longevity. While the loss of friendships and relationships at this stage is predictable, indeed even inevitable, empirical evidence showing that a sense of belonging at this age has a positive impact on physical and psychological wellbeing is often ignored (see Chapter 3; McLaren et al., 2013; Novotney, 2019).

The most effective interventions to address a lack of belonging in older adults are through rebuilding social networks or re-establishing social connectedness (Price, 2015). Researchers have tended to tackle this by providing opportunities for older people to join groups; even the seemingly simple intervention of playing video games in a group has been speculated to have promising implications for a sense of belonging (Chesler et al., 2015).

Community integration has also been found to be positively correlated with successful ageing (Peralta & Moreno, 2019). In one study, seniors integrated into suburban areas tended to view belonging through multiple lenses (Jakubec et al., 2019):

- A feeling (e.g. feeling attached, comforted, accepted, etc.)
- A sense of knowing (e.g. being informed of what is happening in the community)
- A state of being (e.g. connection to others and the community)
- The act of doing (e.g. activities like attending meetings and social gatherings).

These perspectives on belonging clearly depart from the conventional idea that a sense of belonging can be achieved only by being a part of a group, and this apparent flexibility in the human understanding of belonging has the potential to open broader avenues for interventions.

PHYSICAL HEALTH FOR OLDER ADULTS

Having a sense of belonging to groups is also beneficial for physical health. A considerable amount of research has demonstrated the health benefits of social connectedness for reduced mortality (Holt-Lunstad et al., 2010), improved recovery rates following disease (Cohen & Janicki-Deverts, 2009) and improved immune functioning (Cacioppo et al., 2011). A sense of belonging has been found, in general, to be a predictor of health, comparable in significance to a nutritious diet and exercise (Jetten et al., 2009). A lack of social connection is reported to be a health risk factor on par with smoking, obesity and high blood pressure. It significantly increases both the risk of death (Jetten et al., 2009) and mental health concerns (Seeman, 1996).

Bernadette Boden-Albala and colleagues (2005) evaluated the resistance of older people to secondary stroke, heart attack or death following an initial stroke, examining a variety of risk factors, including physical inactivity and coronary heart disease. The findings demonstrated that the greatest risk factor for participants was social isolation. Socially isolated people were twice as likely to have a secondary stroke as those reporting to have strong social relationships. They had worse outcomes overall, while membership in multiple groups was the best predictor of successful stroke recovery and rehabilitation. Haslam and colleagues (2008) demonstrated that stroke sufferers who reported multiple group memberships before their initial stroke also reported better recovery outcomes. Participants who belonged to groups were more resilient to the effects associated with stroke and had a greater sense of wellbeing.

A sense of belonging to groups appears to be particularly important for health and wellbeing across the lifespan, and when opportunities to belong are absent – for example, in the case of social rejection – there can be significant implications for psychological and physical health, as we will see in the next chapter.

4

REJECTION

A feeling of rejection can dramatically undermine our sense of belonging and can, at the same time, create not only immense emotional anguish but also mimic the experience of physical pain. Our desire to belong is so pervasive that a fear of being rejected and not belonging can determine how we navigate our day-to-day life choices and decisions. This chapter will discuss why people are rejected and possible responses to rejection. It will examine the pain of rejection and underscore the devastating impact that rejection can have on our lives.

A FEAR OF NOT BELONGING

Do you dread public speaking? Does the mere thought of standing on a stage in front of an audience strike at your inner core? Perhaps you can portray an air of confidence to get the job done, despite knowing deep down that you are masking an underlying anxiety? Most of us fear public speaking to a greater or lesser degree, but we rarely stop and ask ourselves why.

As we make our way through life, we tread a careful, some-times-tortuous path navigating between unspoken norms and trying not to overstep the boundaries of acceptable social interaction. We modify our remarks, gestures and actions to ensure our behaviour is acceptable for the context, group, culture or community in which we find ourselves. This desire to fit in, and the lengths most of us take to make ourselves acceptable to others, is natural and one of the defining characteristics of life for most humans.

Public speaking can be so frightening because it often seems like a perfect platform for experiencing a radical and mass rejection, with all the consequent threat that has for our cherished sense of belonging to others. When asked why people hate public speaking, the reasons most people give are grounded in concerns about how others might respond: we worry about being laughed at, ridiculed, embarrassed or made to look stupid. It isn't the speaking itself that is scary; it's how the crowd might react.

The truth is, in modern contexts at least, audiences rarely react in ways that are personally negative when someone is speaking. But we nevertheless carry that fear in us as something primal, a worry rooted in humanity's earliest days, when rejection by the group normally meant a lonely and miserable death. These concerns about rejection and exclusion can manifest in all sorts of circumstances. We might hesitate to share an honest appraisal of an event or situation, preferring to tell a white lie to maintain the status quo rather than risk a social breach. Or we might not want to give our opinions in front of a group out of fear that people will think less of us. Our need for belonging can thus exert a strong influence over the way we engage with others and can be a powerful controller of our behaviour.

Rejection is a roadblock to belonging. But why does rejection occur, and why does it so deeply inform our day-to-day behaviour? One of the reasons is that most of us crave a degree of predictability and certainty from others. Uncertainty about how others will respond can lead us to be wary about people, especially those we do not know well and those who fall outside the groups to which we belong. Social psychologists distinguish between *ingroups* and *outgroups*, with the ingroup being the group that we identify as being a member of and the outgroup the group that we do not identify with. The possibility of rejection from the ingroup thus appears as a threat to the stability and certainty of the individual. But in a bitter irony, research has also shown that due to the dynamics of group identity, simply being a member of an outgroup can be a source of rejection. Rejection can thus be feared both because it can result in potential future exclusion and because it can result in a continuation of current exclusion.

OUTGROUPS

Research has suggested that the effects of rejection are felt more strongly by those who are members of social outgroups. These groups can be characterised by a range of features. Some large outgroups consist of people who identify as belonging to racial minorities or who identify as sexually or gender diverse. Ingroup and outgroup membership can also depend on conformity to social norms, so behaviours, attributes or abilities that deviate from what is considered to be normative can also signal outgroup membership (Harrist & Bradley, 2002; Steger & Kashdan, 2009). People with mental health issues or physical disabilities are also frequently treated as belonging to outgroups, and they thus experience rejection on the basis of these characteristics (Steger & Kashdan, 2009).

Ingroup or outgroup membership is not a simple binary attribute. The rejection–identification model proposes that the harmful effects of stigma can be mediated when members of the stigmatised group strengthen their identity through relating to one another and recognising themselves as belonging to a group with a positive identity, whether or not these align with the majority of the mainstream culture. One example is provided by Bogart and colleagues (2018), who explored disability pride, the belief that a disability identity should be positive and uplifting, thus contributing to group solidarity and creating a positive outgroup identity. In this research, stigma had a profound effect on disability pride. However, those who have many or even most of the majority ingroup characteristics can still find themselves in outgroups in given social contexts – for example, a white man who is generally treated well as an ingroup member of society because of his race and gender but who is socially rejected in his workplace. Sometimes ingroup and outgroup membership is contextual.

Whereas some people are rejected on the basis of stereotypes and heuristics, others may behave in a way that makes it difficult for other people to connect with them. Those who are socially anxious, depressed, withdrawn or even inherently shy can also be vulnerable to rejection because connecting with them can be harder and can require more effort on the part of the other person or group (Steger & Kashdan, 2009). In some cases, this can cause a vicious cycle of negativity, with rejections leading to a deepening of the negative feelings that initially contributed to the condition. People with chronic physical illnesses may also be unable to maintain social contact with others, due to health impairments that limit their ability to interact or even to leave the house. When this occurs, the people around them may make less effort of their own to maintain contact or make negative attributions concerning the ill person's behaviour (i.e. concluding that they are uninterested in interacting). Ultimately, when social interaction is impaired over time, others often simply give up.

MALADAPTIVE BEHAVIOUR

Disruptive behaviour can be another common cause for rejection. This may mean behaviour that is aggressive, unpredictable, impulsive or socially undesirable in some other way. When behaviour of this sort departs too far from social norms, it can frequently lead others to avoid or exclude the disruptive individual. In a recent study, Ciuhan (2018) found a strong relationship between aggressive behaviours in children and their rejection by other children, who take distancing measures simply to avoid potential harm. Psychological interventions offer some hopeful possibilities for responding to this type of rejection. Clinicians and teachers can teach emotional regulation, anger management and social skills to the child displaying aggressive behaviour, while the teaching of acceptance and tolerance more broadly can have a positive effect on the children on both sides of the equation.

Interestingly, if intuitively unsurprisingly, parental rejection has been found to predict maladaptive behaviour in children (Putnick et al., 2015). For children experiencing parental rejection, school is sometimes the only place where they have the potential to be safe and cared for. Yet, maladaptive behaviour can also exclude children from a healthy and positive school experience (and from school altogether). This is a cause for particular concern because children who have experienced parental rejection need to belong to school more than most and yet the presence of maladaptive behaviours can be a source of exclusion for them – from peers, but also their school. Such situations often involve immense dedication, planning, support and patience from school staff. Often, unless they can be assisted in developing prosocial behavioural patterns compatible with acceptance by their peers, children in this situation run the risk of going through childhood without feeling that they belong anywhere.

BEHAVIOUR AND PHYSICAL CHARACTERISTICS

Almost half of all people who have reported rejection do not display maladaptive behaviours. Many people who are rejected have a characteristic or trait that departs from the social norm in some way, but they are not necessarily maladaptive. Physical characteristics or behaviours that are not maladaptive but are considered unusual or strange are common causes for rejection (Harrist & Bradley, 2002). In contrast to maladaptive behaviours, such as those involving aggression, it is harder to provide training or interventions to address behaviours that may not be intrinsically problematic and that may, in fact, be inherent characteristics of the individual. Examples that can fall into this category include behaviours with their roots in cultures or ethnicities that differ from the majority, racial attributes, such as differences in skin colour, characteristics associated with a disability and even an individual's perceived lack of physical attractiveness (Harrist & Bradley, 2002). These attributes need not only depart from the majority. Having a different skin colour, for instance, can increase the likelihood of rejection even within a racial group, and issues surrounding appearance can be further intensified for girls. Representations of diversity in the mainstream media are extremely important for this reason. Approaches that target peoples' biases, attitudes and prejudices can help those who would otherwise be rejected to feel included and can normalise their position in society. This can be particularly important for children with a disability.

Rejection on the grounds of disability is perhaps at its most overt in the schoolyard. As much as many schools strive to build inclusive cultures, children with disabilities often experience persistent rejection. In her example, Broomhead (2019) found that children ages five and six with a disability had at least one friendship but had fewer friends than their peers. They were also less socially accepted and, as a result, were isolated from the mainstream and from their typically developing peers.

One concerning observation from research into rejection is that levels of rejection appear to be higher if the individual's difference appears to be under their control, such as obesity. Research indicates that people with obesity are often subject to negative experiences because of stereotypes associated with their condition. These stereotypes can be reinforced, and the negative consequences intensified, by the media's propagation of standards that are unrealistic for the vast majority of the population. Albano and colleagues (2019) conducted a systematic review of studies concerning the interpersonal difficulties encountered by individuals with obesity. The results showed that individuals with obesity report greater interpersonal stress and lower quality of social life than those with a healthy weight, as well as being subject to increased rates of bullying and teasing. An explanation of these findings may be related to social rejection from the perception that the individuals with obesity are in control of their circumstances and brought the situation upon themselves.

Social stereotyping of those who have addiction problems provides another example. For centuries, common negative perceptions of people with addiction have led to rejection, ostracism, the erection of barriers to help and the consequent growth of unhealthy subcultures to which addicts can feel a sense of belonging. Possibly the most pervasive and misleading of these stereotypes is the myth that addiction is a choice for the individual and is therefore controllable. What we often fail to acknowledge as a society is that addiction, in any form, is frequently a mechanism that masks an underlying condition or a deeper psychological problem.

Dr. Bruce Alexander, a psychologist and researcher from Vancouver, has argued an alternative view of drug addiction since the 1970s. He and his colleagues from Simon Fraser University in British Columbia hypothesised that drugs themselves are not the cause of addiction, rather addiction is triggered by the living conditions and current state of the person using the drugs. To investigate this hypothesis, they carried out a series of now infamous studies known as *Rat Park*. In these experiments, a rat is isolated and confined in a cage. In the first few trials, the rat in the cage is presented with two choices of water: plain water or water laced with either morphine or cocaine (Alexander et al., 1985; Alexander et al., 1978). The researchers observed that the isolated rats would repeatedly choose the drugged water, even if they incurred withdrawal symptoms. Also, when the plain water was sweetened, the rats continued to choose the drugged water. These results led Alexander and his colleagues to devise an alternative trial to examine whether the decision to choose the drugged water related to the rat's deprivation of other rats. To do this, they built Rat Park, a large cage in which approximately 20 rats resided. The rats were provided with a wide range of options for activities and play, were given a variety of food choices and were left with ample space for mating. The rats in Rat Park were still able to freely choose between plain water and drugged water, but for the most part, selected the plain water instead. The findings provided considerations for drug use and especially the potential influence of the social environment.

Peter Cohen, a Dutch sociologist, has claimed that drug addiction is a myth and has advocated for many years that we should not conceptualise it through the lens of crime. Instead, he contends, it is a problem that has its origins in human connection. The assumption that the origins of addiction lie in a lack of social connection has been applied at the national level in Portugal, with remarkable results. After decades of failing to obtain desirable results when treating addiction as a crime, the Portuguese government decided to approach it in a radically different manner. The programme involved decriminalising drug possession and reallocating all relevant funds towards the goal of reconnecting people experiencing drug addiction with society (Felix et al., 2017). Unsurprisingly, the policy change yielded positive results with problematic drug use declining by up to 10%.

The evidence just discussed strongly suggests that we need to re-evaluate our social prejudices towards people. The lens of belonging offers up a powerful way of viewing individuals that acknowledges that human beings are social creatures and that they thus have an innate need to bond and form connections with others.

REPUTATION

According to Harrist and colleagues, another reason why people are rejected is reputation. When someone has been rejected in the past, the associated reputation of having been rejected can be enduring and pervasive. In such cases, a *recursion effect* is more likely to occur. A recursion effect takes place when the expectation that a person will behave in a particular way actually serves to promote the expected behaviour (Harrist & Bradley, 2002), further reinforcing the problematic reputation as a consequence. Research on social acceptance and perceived social reputations among early adolescents has revealed that social acceptance is directly associated with perceptions of popularity, rejection and aggressive reputation (Badaly et al., 2012). A lack of social acceptance based on reputation alone can have a profound and enduring negative effect on future interpersonal relationships. A pattern of rejection and recursion based on reputation can be persistent and may last for a person's entire lifetime. This, of course, creates an important rationale for intervening early, especially at school.

NOT BELONGING HURTS

Moieni and Eisenberger (2018) point out that the common school-yard saying "Sticks and stones may break my bones, but words will never hurt me" is far from true (p. 203). Years of research in psychology and neuroscience have shown what most of us already knew intuitively: social exclusion hurts, and the pain is real rather than metaphorical. Indeed, we now know that the response to social pain in our neural processing is similar in significant ways to the neural response to physical pain (Eisenberger et al., 2003) and that both social and physical pain share overlapping neural processes. This similarity is reflected in the physicalised language that we use to describe emotional pain: "She stabbed me in the back" or "It was like a knife in my heart". Interpersonal conflict, a falling out with a friend, a broken romantic relationship or unrequited love can affect us deeply, not only on an emotional level but also on a physical level. As a result, we might fall ill, become depressed, lose our appetite or actually feel an ache in our heart. Our physiological systems are threatened, and our immune systems can be compromised (Slavich, 2020).

A classic experiment called Cyberball has been used to examine the physical impact of rejection (Williams & Jarvis, 2006). In this computer-generated game, participants believe they are playing with other players. However, the "other players" are actually controlled by the researcher, who is able to manipulate the speed of the game and the frequency at which the player is included in the ball toss or left out. When the game starts, the participant is involved in the ball-tossing sequence but is eventually left out – observing the other players toss the ball between themselves. Participants are asked how they feel and the responses invariably represent rejection, ostracism and a decline in their sense of belonging (Williams et al., 2000). When the experiences of the Cyberball game have been observed in neuroimaging studies, the responses from participants at a neural level show that the event of being excluded shares the same hallmark neural activity as physical pain (Eisenberger et al., 2003).

OBSERVING PAIN

Even observing the social pain of others can cause feelings of pain in the observer, to varying degrees. Interestingly, it appears that similar brain circuits are activated regardless of whether someone is suffering personally from social pain or they are observing the pain in someone else. For example, seeing a loved one suffer from bullying, social exclusion or a breakup can hurt us just as much as it hurts them. However, some research has shown that even a commercial or an advertisement can cause us physical pain and empathy towards strangers (Lin et al., 2013). This may be why some people avoid empathy. Given that our brains are hardwired to retain negative information more easily than positive information, exposure to pain or traumatic events may contribute to chronic stress. However, it is also possible that this sympathetic pain plays a protective role, by creating a warning signal in the observer about a danger they should seek to avoid. This sympathetic fellow feeling also helps us to connect with one another, thus supporting a range of prosocial behaviours and contributing to the development of communities.

REJECTION AND DEATH

It may be possible to even go so far as to draw a connection between rejection and death. Some researchers have found a strong link between social isolation and early death, for instance. Holt-Lunstad and colleagues (2015) conducted a meta-analysis of 70 studies that examined more than three million older adults and found that social isolation increased a person's likelihood of dying from disease by 29%. In the synthesis, studies that explored death by suicide or accident were excluded from the meta-analysis. However, given the strong implication of social rejection on mental health, suicide is also an important consideration when evaluating risk factors associated with death.

In many parts of the world, suicide is a leading cause of death for young people aged between 15 and 44. In fact, these young people are more likely to die from taking their own life than they are to perish in a motor vehicle accident (Kinchin & Doran, 2018). Poor school networks, bullying and depleted coping resources are predictive factors for suicidal ideation and suicide attempts (Olcoń et al., 2017; Wyman et al., 2019). Posie wrote pseudonymously for the website *White Wreath*, an Australian suicide and mental health charity. Her personal story of suicide discusses how her lack of belonging led to suicidal ideation:

> My life had been so "abnormal" from the time I was a young child. I came from a European family – which made me "feel" different. I always felt like a misfit, like I didn't "belong" anywhere, like I was adopted, and I was so extremely sensitive and desperate to please. I remember being 16 and thinking "I'm too weak for this world; it's too evil, how will I ever survive it" – I just didn't think I could cope, even back then.
>
> (White Wreath Association Ltd, 2020)

While further research is needed, there are strong reasons to look further into the possibility of a link between rejection and early death.

REJECT DOCUMENTARY

To highlight the risks associated with rejection, including suicide, Ruth Thomas Suh created the documentary *Reject*. Investigating social rejection, bullying and the dark side of not belonging, the documentary was possibly the first piece of mainstream media to highlight how critical rejection can be for people's life trajectories and created an important platform for the sharing of research on the topic. Ruth, in her director's statement, wrote,

> My goal in making *Reject* is to provoke an informed discussion about the serious – sometimes lethal – consequences of interpersonal rejection, which comes in the guise of bullying, parental neglect and abuse, racial bias, and other forms, across all age

groups. My hope is that an exploration of the science of social rejection and an introduction to possible solutions can encourage educators, public agencies and others to institute policies and programs that promote behaviours of acceptance, tolerance and inclusion. These include improving child health and welfare in schools by adding social and emotional learning to common-core curricula and de-stigmatizing mental health problems. Scientific breakthroughs continue to reveal our fundamentally social nature, and show us we all have a profound human need to belong.

Discussing belonging and rejection on mainstream platforms is critical to raising public awareness about the importance of belonging and the damaging effects of rejection on people throughout their lives, and it may offer important implications for suicide prevention in the future.

REJECTION AS A FORM OF PUNISHMENT

Possibly one of the most compelling cases for the adversity of rejection is our tendency to use it as a form of punishment. Steeped in a rich history, early tribal groups would use isolation from the group as a punishment that almost invariably resulted in death. More recently, solitary confinement provides another example where even pews in jails are often separated by dividers that deny incarcerated church attendees access to other people, in a place otherwise devoted to community and belonging.

In schools and in homes, children are denied social interaction for short periods through punishments, such as time outs or even planned ignoring. These are often viewed as more modern and child-friendly replacements for physical punishments, but they to some degree represent the removal of social interaction. More extreme examples of social isolation as a form of discipline have been reported in some schools with highly restrictive practices, using cages and isolation rooms to manage the behaviour of children with autism spectrum disorder (ASD). One teenage girl with ASD was placed in an isolation booth more than 240 times between grades 7 and 11 in a school in England. The trauma associated with the isolation booth caused her communication skills to regress and led to the experience of panic attacks, suicidal ideation and depression (Haynes, 2019). Similarly, the solitary confinement of prisoners has been proven to have significant detrimental psychological effects, including social fear, clinical depression, psychosis and suicidal behaviour (Arrigo & Bullock, 2008).

Rejection, social isolation and exclusion from groups are painful experiences, which explains why they are so readily used as punishment. However, what is far less well understood is exactly why it is that isolation, social exclusion and the denial of social belonging can have such a profound impact on us, an impact that can create serious problems for our psychological and physical health (see Chapters 2 and 3).

5

BELONGING IN AN AGE OF TECHNOLOGY

As a society, while many of us have the ability to connect to more and more people in an increasing variety of ways, the decline in face-to-face communication also means that fewer social opportunities are available for some of those who rely on more traditional forms of interactions (Drago, 2015). Are these changes affecting our social satisfaction and leading to increases in the number of people feeling lonely? Are our social skills suffering as a result? Less-direct exposure to other people and fewer opportunities to experience and observe them at first hand could have a particularly large impact on young people (Goodman-Deane et al., 2016). The connections we have today with family, friends and neighbours are unavoidably shaped by rapid developments in technology. But is technology helping or hampering our sense of belonging? This chapter engages with this question and discusses new research into how rapid changes in technology are influencing our social interactions and sense of belonging.

WHEN TECHNOLOGY DIVIDES

On the 14 March 2019, a 28-year-old shooter opened fire on worshipers at two mosques in Christchurch, New Zealand, leaving 50 people dead and scores of others injured. Technology played a central role in these horrifying events. Not only did the shooter livestream the shootings via Facebook, but he also used other social media sites, including Instagram and Twitter, to post videos, articles and Internet memes that pedalled a toxic far-right agenda of social exclusion and hatred. A manifesto for his actions, criticising racial integration and migration, also circulated online. One of the most disturbing outcomes was the amplification of his message by news and media outlets who broadcast the video stream in the wake of the event, giving his views and actions a global reach that they would have otherwise lacked.

Technology is no longer just an extension of our lives, like a porch built onto a house. It now forms the bricks and mortar of our daily existence. Technology is integrated with all manner of typical behaviours and is used as part of our everyday habits. It intersects our relationships and has an inevitable impact on human development. Children now grow up in environments in which their parents spend far more time in front of screens than did previous generations. Work and domestic labours have always drawn the attention of parents away from their children, but modern technology poses a host of new challenges. Not only does it encourage an "always-on" attitude towards working practices, bringing the workplace home into more households than ever before, but the feed of alerts, texts, message group responses, social media updates, news stories and so on being constantly fed directly into the hands of adults provides additional distractions.

This new environment throws up a range of important questions. What is the impact on children of parents checking their work emails while their child plays alone? How does additional parental screen time affect the social development of children? Are effects compounded if the children are also watching a screen at the same time? Tempting as it is to respond to these questions based on intuitions about negative consequences, it is important to let the research speak for itself. In fact, there do seem to be at least some positive outcomes for parent–child relationships from the increasing prevalence of technology, especially with respect to flexibility with work for some, which may mean more time spent at home. Nevertheless, it seems that parental screen time may indeed have an influence on the amount of time that children spend on their screens, with some studies finding a correlation between parents who spend a lot of time on screen media and children who do likewise (Lauricella et al., 2015).

Screen time also appears to be connected to socioeconomic status. Children from more affluent backgrounds are reportedly using screens less, while children from lower-income families are spending more time on screens (Tandon et al., 2012). This raises the troubling question of whether the excessive use of technology might become responsible for creating yet another disadvantage for those from less affluent backgrounds.

HOW MUCH SCREEN TIME DO PARENTS HAVE OUTSIDE WORK ON AVERAGE?

Parents report as spending as many as nine to 11 hours on screen media each day, with over 80% of that time related to personal use. While this number may seem extremely high, it becomes easier to comprehend when we consider the extent to which we are surrounded by screens in our everyday lives. Not only do most of us carry smartphones, but almost everywhere we go there are also tablets, computers and televisions within easy reach. We do not just use these devices when we are sitting still either – they are constant companions on the go as well, and we have come to rely on them for everything from mapping a journey in our car to summoning up a recipe in the kitchen. We text partners and friends as we walk, and we use email to let people know when we are running late. We may not all be using our devices constantly for nine or more hours each day, but many of us are using them much more than we might first think.

You do not need to look too far afield to find research that raises concerns about the heavy use of electronic devices and the consequent high number of hours of screen time. Studies have identified issues related to a range of negative outcomes for children, such as increases in attention-seeking behaviour, sleep disturbances, language delays, and physical inactivity and impediments to executive functioning, social skill development and school readiness (Richards et al., 2010; Parent et al., 2016; Duch et al., 2013; Christofaro et al., 2016). Technology effects the way we socialise, and this influences how we bond with others and develop a sense of belonging.

WHAT EFFECT CAN SCREEN TIME HAVE ON CHILDREN'S SENSE OF BELONGING WITH THEIR PARENTS?

On the one hand, technology affords us a range of benefits, such as the ability to work remotely or from home, which hold out the possibility of more family-friendly lives. But these potential benefits also come with consequences. While it may please some to work at home surrounded by their family, many others feel additional burdens from increased expectations and demands associated with the assumption that they are available 24/7, and there are in turn inevitable distractions from family and home life. For some, at least, being able to spend more time at home does not equate with having more time for family life. In addition to work burdens, distractions caused by digital media, and particularly smartphones, can often interrupt moments that have the potential for allowing genuine connections between parents and children (Kushlev & Dunn, 2018).

Studies have demonstrated that parents feel less connected to their children the more that parents use their smartphones (Kushlev & Dunn, 2018). Other research has shown that a sense of connection can be interrupted during parent–child learning experiences, with negative consequences for learning outcomes. Indeed, it is easy to see why incidental learning opportunities could easily be hampered by the parent's attention being divided between their child and their smartphone. Unsurprisingly, some children have reported feeling that they actually have to compete against a smartphone for their parents' attention (McDaniel & Radesky, 2018). This issue can be particularly challenging for parents who juggle multiple roles.

ARE THERE ANY POSITIVE EFFECTS OF PARENTAL SCREEN TIME?

At the most basic level, when electronic devices and screen time are used as tools to improve work efficiency and thus free up time to connect and foster relationships with their children, they have a clear, indirect positive effect. But there are also more direct contexts in which benefits can be detected.

CHILD-CENTRED PROGRAMMES

Significant positive effects can also emerge from screen media, and these can make it hard to offer straightforward guidelines about appropriate levels of screen time. For example, there is evidence to suggest that from around two years of age, age-appropriate television programmes that are conscientiously constructed can have educational benefits and provide increased learning opportunities (Mares & Pan, 2013). This has been found to be especially true for programmes that encourage imaginative/pretend play.

VIEWING TOGETHER

Some benefits also derive from parental guidance during a child's interaction with screen media (e.g. when parents view and interact with screen media together with their child). In the case of appropriately guided interactions, research has found some degree of benefit for the promotion of early literacy skills (Strouse et al., 2013). There is also an emerging body of literature that supports the value of certain wellbeing apps on smartphones and tablets, which can help teach children a range of skills related to coping and emotional regulation (Morris et al., 2010; Bakker & Rickard, 2018). However, how these benefits relate specifically to a sense of belonging to family relationships is a question that requires further research.

Other examples of the use of electronic devices can also create moments of meaningful connection, especially when the screen is shared and/or used as a relationship-building tool. A parent's talking and reminiscing with their child over baby photos on a smartphone is just one example of the productive and positive use of screen media. In many cases, context is key to whether an interaction will be an opportunity to build belonging or whether it will distract from belonging.

ADOLESCENTS AND TECHNOLOGY

Once upon a time, not that long ago, adolescents would sit glued to fixed-line telephones, to the great frustration of their parents and anyone trying to call. These days, however, it seems that written communication is preferred over verbal communication. Some analysis of modern communications suggests that written communications are going through a process of rapid change and condensation. In the context of a text, email or instant message, brevity is often key; whole sentences are sometimes reduced to a few consonants and vowels, and words are often done away with entirely in favour of an acronym, symbol or emoji. And while this way of communicating is efficient, we have to wonder whether this style of communicating for young people is allowing them to build the connections they need to fulfil their need to belong and equip them with the necessary skills to build relationships with others in the future.

The effects of technology on adolescent wellbeing may not be as severe as the media frequently leads us to believe (Orben & Przybylski, 2018). However, caution is necessary here: the research is still catching up with contemporary habits, and we do not yet have the kind of data that will allow us to understand the true implications of technology on our sense of belonging to others and to groups. There is already a broad intuitive awareness among the public that the effects of technology can be profound, and this has led more and more people to experiment with the idea of the "digital detox". Increasing numbers of apps are now available to block or limit the use of social media sites, while other tools, such as greyscale filters, can be used to make screen time less appealing. More direct measures can also be taken, with some schools going as far as to enact complete bans on the use of mobile phones on their grounds.

We know that excessive screen time or the compulsion to check our phones for updates can disrupt our ability to connect with others. However, the long-term implications for adolescents on their changing behavioural patterns have not yet been determined. But it is not all doom and gloom. While some of the consequences of modern technology may have concerning implications for the average teenager, even the dangers have the potential to make us more aware of how young people connect with others. For instance, simply reflecting on what we risk losing can lead us to focus more consciously on vital elements of a relationship – especially between parent/caregiver and a young person or the relationships between teenagers.

Another concern that has been raised about the effects of digital technology on young people is the potential of technology to reduce opportunities for the attainment and development of social skills. Turkle (2011) suggests that connecting with people through technological rather than physical means may result in a loss of the types of social skills required for face-to-face interaction. It is reasonable to expect that children who spend large amounts of time on electronic devices could have more social difficulties during later adolescence.

In the absence of research on the topic, many schools have banned the use of mobile phones during class and break times, and some have banned their use on school grounds altogether. These decisions have polarised the academic community, some of whom believe that in the absence of electronic devices, young people will not learn the necessary skills to use them appropriately. School leaders and teachers have anecdotally reported that students are spending less time looking at their devices and more time interacting with peers. What happens beyond the school gates, however, is not under the direct control of schools.

THE BROADER ISSUE

In *Bowling Alone: The Collapse and Revival of American Community*, Robert D. Putnam (2000) writes that the connections we have with family, friends and neighbours are shaped by rapid developments in technology. Putman notes a decline in *social capital* – that is, the value of social networks that arise from social intercourse with other individuals and families. Putman acknowledges that the Internet is a useful tool for connecting *physically distant* people. However, he also asks whether access to technology might challenge the possibility of forming genuine relationships and building communities: "is virtual social capital itself a contradiction of terms?" (p. 170). And he asks whether technology has contributed to a trend in deteriorating social connectedness. These questions were prescient when he wrote his book 20 years ago and have become ever more urgent in the years since. While there is a consensus that feeling a sense of belonging has a positive impact on physical health and wellbeing, further investigation is needed to help us understand the factors which influence belonging itself, particularly with respect to technology.

A MODERN SENSE OF COMMUNITY

A sense of community in the modern world need not be limited by physical contact or geography. Some relational communities are not linked to a locality but are based instead on a shared interest or purpose. McMillan and Chavis (1986) describe a psychological sense of community as a "feeling that members have of belonging, a feeling that members matter to one another and to the group, and a shared faith that members' needs will be met through their commitment to be together" (p. 9).

Research into the structures and the processes underlying online communities and groups is growing. Social media enables individuals to find a smaller subset of the broader community which they identify with and to which they feel they belong. Examples can be found in the formation of online groups around a particular hobby or support groups that enable people to come together around a common issue, adversity or diagnosis. However, few researchers have studied whether online communities create the same type of belonging that we feel when we connect to groups in the physical world. The qualities and actions of online groups appear to be like those of offline communities, but although social networks share some features of offline communities (e.g. exchanging resources and social support), more research is needed to investigate the full benefits of belonging towards an online community group. It may be that online social networks can serve different functions. For example, casual membership in a social networking site to "keep in contact with friends" might provoke different forms of cognition and different effects than would membership in an online support group or forum designed for individuals with cancer.

In late 2017, Katie Gilchrist (@mysenseoftumour), a senior consultant, was diagnosed with an acoustic neuroma brain tumour. In 2019, she underwent surgery and struggled to find the right social support networks online, so she built her own on Instagram. The following is Katie's story:

> When I was first diagnosed, I went looking online for support networks and information others with the same condition had shared. To my surprise, what I found was a web of negativity. As a way of coping (and also to share my story with others) I created an Instagram account and a blog where I have documented my story from day one. Now with a bit of a following, I have created a community of support for not only myself but others with the same condition.

You can read Katie's blog at https://mysenseoftumour.com.

One explanation for Katie's experience may be that different platforms provide different benefits. Pittman and Reich (2016) found that image-based visual platforms such as Instagram and Snapchat have users with less self-reported loneliness and increased happiness than users of more text-based platforms. It may be possible that when we view other photos of people, we are more likely to have the feeling that another person, a friend, is really there.

PERCEPTION OF FRIENDSHIP

Turkle (2011) has suggested that the difference between online communities and offline communities may be rooted in the fact that connecting with people over the Internet gives us only the perception of friendship; we are in contact but we remain physically alone. Jones (1997) suggests that some online groups are *virtual communities*, whereas others are *virtual settlements*, with frequent changes in members and consequently less emotional connection. Researchers have also noted that "heavy Internet use" can alienate people and reduce social contact (e.g. Beard, 2002; Erdoğan, 2008; Weiser, 2001), thereby hindering face-to-face relationships, regardless of the possible value of online communities.

Other scholars have used cross-cultural perspectives to examine perceptions of friendships. Sheldon and colleagues (2017) compared Croatian users and American users of Instagram, finding that Croatian participants reported greater gratification from social media use than did the American participants in the study. The researchers speculated that Croatians were more "we"-focused and Americans more "me"-focused, drawing from individualism vs collectivism thoughts; however, it was also suggested that the Croatian participants perceived their "followers" as friends, whereas American participants were more likely to consider them as "fans".

LONELINESS AND TECHNOLOGY

A major concern that has been raised with the increasing prevalence of technology is its negative association with loneliness. Stepanikova and colleagues (2010) examined digital tools and found that people who spent increased time on the Internet – using chat rooms, messaging groups and newsgroups, for example – felt lonelier than those who spent less time or no time at all. Email neither increased nor decreased wellbeing. While certain studies have shown that the Internet increases loneliness (e.g. Erdoğan, 2008), not all studies have drawn the same conclusion, particularly when investigating certain groups of people. For example, the Internet has actually been shown to decrease feelings of loneliness in people who identify themselves as lonely or shy. Bonetti and colleagues (2010) found that Internet use allowed people who were shy to interact in ways they would not have done in "real life" due to feeling too intimidated. Online groups may, then, provide communities in which shy people can feel emotionally safe.

Studies have also found that people who report feeling lonely may benefit from Internet use, with the research suggesting that increased Internet use can decrease feelings of loneliness and increase social support in real life. Studies have arrived at similar findings when examining Internet use in older and isolated populations (e.g. Khosravi et al., 2016), and people who are considered introverts (Kircaburun & Griffiths, 2018). Kuss and Griffiths (2011) found that extraverts use online platforms to consolidate friendships that already exist, whereas introverts use online networks to create meaningful relationships. There have been further speculations about why social media use may decrease loneliness. Yang (2016) suggests that not all social media use is as passive as it may first appear. In fact, people may use social media as a prelude to social contact. Moreover, social media networks might also remind people about how big their social networks are, even if they are not interacting with them daily.

FINAL THOUGHTS

Given the prevalence of technology in our daily lives, it has never been more important to study its capacity to foster belonging. Research so far has suggested that whether technology detracts from or strengthens our ability to belong is dependent on the context, use and the individual. New technologies change the way we share and consume knowledge but also influence how we socially interact. To really grasp the ongoing effects this kind of technological change has on individuals and society, new research is needed to study not only how the technology itself influences our social interactions and how, in turn, we define belonging, community and advancement but also how we manage and process the speed of the change, the rapid turnover of technologies and the social and cultural change it brings.

6

BELONGING BAD

Belonging is paradoxical in many ways. Belonging to an outgroup, by definition, implies exclusion from an ingroup. However, exclusion from an outgroup does not automatically return an individual to the ingroup. On the contrary, it can often send a person down a path that seeks inclusion and belonging in an outgroup that departs from societal norms in a more extreme way.

Healthy human relationships can offer refuge from the daily trials and tribulations of life. They can help us to cope with challenges, offer valuable social support during times of need and build our sense of purpose and belonging. But for a relationship to provide an effective refuge, there must be a mutual sense of safety and security among those who are brought together. Relationships that lack these two factors will fail to thrive and can be extremely detrimental to wellbeing during childhood and adolescence. When healthy relationships and opportunities to belong are absent, young people will often seek a sense of belonging elsewhere. Indeed, so fundamental is the need to belong that some young people will accept almost anything to secure acceptance for themselves. A sense of belonging somewhere is not always a good thing, and the desire to belong *anywhere* can lead an individual down some potentially dark paths. As we will explore in this chapter, there are plenty of antisocial routes to finding a sense of belonging.

Nichols (2006) argues that belongingness can have both a negative and positive effect. For example, some students may find school to be a positive source of belonging "because of the support they receive from teachers but bad because of friends (or lack thereof), or vice versa" (p. 265). The idea that belonging can be both positive and negative has implications for researchers investigating gang and mob behaviour. Members of these groups may well have a strong sense of belonging, but this belonging often results in negative outcomes. Roffey (2013) has suggested that this tension can be reflected by distinguishing between inclusive belonging and exclusive belonging. Inclusive belonging can be conceptualised as a kind that reaches out to others, whereas exclusive belonging involves attitudes that manifest a sense of superiority or that are directed towards self-protection (Roffey, 2013).

COMMUNITIES IN CULTS

Our drive to interact with others and develop a sense of belonging can lead to questionable choices. As has been discussed elsewhere in this book, one way to form a sense of connection is to be part of a group. And when a sense of belonging is absent or unavailable elsewhere, groups that are typically classified as cults may appear highly appealing. Cults are defined as organisations or groups composed of individuals with common interests and beliefs who are devoted to a leader or object. Studies reveal that most people recruited to join a cult are adolescents and young adults between 18 and 25 years old. Cult membership is also far more common than is often believed. Across the United States, for example, between two million and five million people are affiliated with approximately 2,000 to 5,000 cult groups (Robinson et al., 1997). The designation of a group as "a cult" is almost always an external label, and few people who join such groups consider that the organisation that appeals to them fits into this category. Once they do realise that they have become enmeshed with a group of this type, it can often be extremely difficult to disentangle their lives.

In cults, the indoctrination of people by often influential leaders can serve as a source of what is sometimes called *symbolic interaction*. Symbolic interactionism is a theory that seeks to understand how people construct the symbolic worlds that guide behaviour and shape how we interact with others. According to this approach, the repeated interactions that occur between individuals can be interpreted in terms of the shaping of collective understandings of social contexts. From this perspective, the use of rituals and symbols in cults can be understood as providing meaning and purpose to the interactions and activities that occur. They thus cement membership in the collective by reinforcing shared group mindsets and a common conceptual framework.

While popular ideas of cult membership have tended to be shaped by depictions in entertainment and media that focus on the more extreme departures from social norms, most conversions to cults do not entail any radical alteration of lifestyle. What makes cult membership attractive to the individual is the perception of benefits, such as a sense of security, meaning, purpose and belonging. Cult members can also develop a folie à deux (or shared delusion). Often it is believed that the shared identity and knowledge of cult members sets them apart, and makes them different, from non-members. A recent review of literature on the subject identified the search for a sense of belonging as one of the reasons why many people join cults. Other reasons include the elimination of conflict, frustration, confusion and anxiety. Negative experiences of this sort may motivate people to find alternative social solutions to avoid the undesirable feelings they experience in normal society (Zhang, 2017).

Margaret, with six siblings, was born into a religious sect called the Exclusive Brethren. The following is her story:

> As a child, being a member of this sect provided a great sense of belonging. I could interact daily with multiple relatives and sect friends and there was an open-home approach to visiting. Sect members could drop by our house and school holidays were especially memorable as there was always someone's place

I could walk, cycle or get driven to, to play with other sect family members or go with to some public places. School life at this time was also a happy time. There were no sect children except my siblings at the primary school I attended and I was able to interact with all the children in my class during school hours. When I was 12 and going into my adolescent years, life as I knew it changed. My parents were ex-communicated (for a period of three years) from the sect, for a misdemeanour that they had to be forgiven in order to return to the fold of the sect. This tore my family apart. My two older sisters who were working, thus able to support themselves, left the family home and went to live with a sect member and I, along with my other four siblings, stayed at home with mum and dad. I still belonged in my family, albeit it [was] divided, and within my school group of friends while at school, but all the sect friends I had grown up with and had previously belonged [with] now physically ignored me. This challenged my sense of belonging. I felt like I was in a no-man's land, outcast and punished for my parents' transgression and yet not able to be fully part of my school friends "after-school" community as a non-sect member. The shame of this isolated position initially was too confusing to divulge to my school friends, so I was sometimes untruthful and averted difficult questions in order to stay connected and belong in this group. Being accepted by my school friends allowed me to enjoy my adolescent years and school became my sanctuary.

GANGS AND BELONGING

When we think about group belonging, we usually think about social inclusion, equity, equality, human rights, engagement, tolerance and the embracing of diversity. But in fact, when a prosocial avenue for belonging is not available, individuals strive to meet their needs for belongingness in other fora. The combination of a poor sense of school belonging and living in a low-income neighbourhood with a high crime rate significantly increases the chances of adolescents' and adults' gravitating towards gangs when these two age groups are in search of a sense of belonging that they would otherwise lack (Lenzi et al., 2019).

When we think about gang members, stereotypes often shape our expectations. We imagine a gang member to be violent, antisocial and aggressive and to possess other negative traits and engage in other negative behaviours that are usually at odds with social peace and harmony. Despite the widespread negative connotations of gang membership, many people are still drawn to these groups. So, what do gangs offer that make membership desirable for some people?

Gang culture has existed for centuries as a staple of urban life. Curry (2004) describes a gang as a group of people who collaborate for antisocial reasons usually concerned with criminal behaviour. Street gangs, although arguably less problematic for society than criminal gangs (such as organised syndicates), garner a great deal of attention from the general public, largely driven by the fear they create in their communities due to their visibility. In 2007, the National Youth Gang Center identified approximately 785,000 active street gang members in the United States. In 2011, the National Gang Intelligence Center of the Federal Bureau of Investigation (FBI) recorded more than 33,000 gangs in the country. These gangs vary in type, visibility and membership. Some of the most infamous street gangs are characterised by specific racial profiles, while biker gangs may have a more varied membership but a particularly strong set of visual identifying markers.

When seeking to understand why gang membership can appear attractive, it is useful to consider a historical type of gang that continues to capture the imaginations of children everywhere: pirates. Although pirates still exist today, primarily in the Pacific Ocean and Indian Ocean, we tend to be most familiar with entertaining representations of European pirates from the Age of Sail. The popular makeover these gangs have undergone, which often airbrushes some of the more unpleasant aspects of their activities, helps draw attention to the more attractive features of gang membership. Pirates are represented as outsiders who form a shared sense of belonging around their ability to work as a team in pursuit of collective goals (mostly concerned with pillaging other vessels). A shared social code helped pirate crews to work together in conditions of extreme hardship and to overcome the adversity they faced as individuals beyond the bounds of mainstream society. Considered from this perspective, it is easy to see why membership in such a group would have been attractive to those who would otherwise have had to face the world alone. Group loyalty and mutual aid ran extremely deep in at least some cases: one group of Baltic pirates named themselves the Likedeelers, or "equal sharers", to encapsulate the egalitarian nature of their brotherhood.

Curry (2004) suggests that the sense of belonging fostered by membership in a group apart from society is one of the reasons why people, especially the young, join gangs. She argues that being part of an organised gang gives the individual a sense of belonging similar to that which comes from being part of a family. Research shows that most gang members find patriarchal role models in the gangs to which they belong, something of importance to those with absent fathers (Curry, 2004). Studies show that gang-involved youth often have backgrounds that involve personal and interpersonal challenges in either their family or their community (Van Ngo et al., 2017). Through membership in a gang, they gain both a positive image of themselves and a sense of social identity (Van Ngo et al., 2017). Youth who feel that they do not belong to their school may also find a sense of safety and social salvation in a gang. It is possible that those who join gangs feel worthless and powerless, and gang membership helps to alleviate these feelings. It is perhaps because of evidence like this that some parts of the world have taken to legalising street gang membership. The Ecuadorian government, for example, has legalised street gangs since 2008. Ethnographic research exploring street gangs living in Ecuador has found them to be a source of social inclusion. The government's policy to reject models of gang repression has resulted in a marked decrease in gang-related violence across the country (Brotherton & Gude, 2020).

Not all gangs are focused on violence, seizing power and breaking the law. For many gang members, the main role of the group is to provide an alternative source of the safety and security that a typical family can offer. Some teenage gangs, such as the Greasers depicted in S. E. Hinton's *The Outsiders*, are relatively benign and simply provide a way for those who are otherwise excluded to feel a sense of belonging and to find comfort in conformity within the group.

TERRORISM AND RADICALISATION

Research by Lyons-Padilla and colleagues (2015) examining Muslim immigrants found that there is no one typical personality or psychopathology shared by terrorists. Nevertheless, the research showed that some people were more at risk of radicalisation than others. Immigrants who reject their heritage culture and do not identify with the culture in which they are presently living, who feel marginalised or ostracised, or have experienced discrimination are at a greater risk of becoming radicalised and taking part in terrorist activities. Many people who join extremist groups have themselves experienced significant personal trauma, loss, neglect or abuse. It may be that they turn to extremism because the group offers a way to find a sense of meaning, purpose and even self-worth (Lyons-Padilla et al., 2015). In other cases, individuals may have been excluded from society and are unable to find a sense of belonging through joining traditional outside groups.

Radicalisation is the process that leads to participation in antisocial acts or norm-violating behaviours through the development of extremist ideals. Social psychologists have enumerated three essential components that are needed for radicalisation to take place: the universal human need to live a meaningful life, the narrative and the community (Kruglanski et al., 2014). The community in this context is a group of people who justifies the *narrative* or the story they have told themselves about the injustices, inequality and immorality occurring around them. The validity of the narrative is by itself seen as enough to justify the actions of community members. Accordingly, if the narrative is accepted, then committing violent crimes is not just warranted but deemed reasonable. People who join radical movements do so in the belief that what they are doing is both valuable and worth fighting for. The belief of the individual that their undertakings are worthwhile satisfies the desire to live with a purpose. Often, a more in-depth reflection on and understanding of people who join terrorist groups can lead us to see that the primary motivation for their actions is the psychological longing to matter and to be a significant part of something.

Young people are more vulnerable to radicalisation than those belonging to other age groups. Studies have shown that adolescence – the developmental phase itself – is a risk factor for radicalisation since it is a stage that can be characterised by identity confusion and reformation (Campelo et al., 2018). Identity development and confusion are often central to a young person's radicalisation. As a result, young people who experience uncertainty about their social identity are more susceptible to converting their beliefs and behaviours, adopting new identities as a means to avoid or to circumvent being estranged and ostracised. It is perhaps unsurprising, then, that young people who do not feel a sense of belonging to school are the most at risk of radicalised behaviour or extremist group membership (Hogg et al., 2010).

In addition, the psychological vulnerabilities that are particularly prevalent in youths – such as personal uncertainty, perceived unfairness, traumatic experiences like childhood abandonment and other environmental factors such as family dysfunction and peer pressure – make them more susceptible to radicalisation (Campelo et al., 2018). By belonging to radical movements, young people may find a sense of belonging, security, identity, purpose and meaning. The need to belong does not imply a diminishment of the genuine beliefs of most members that they are fighting for an important cause or advocating for the sovereignty of a particular righteous group. Rather, it provides a psychological scaffolding that can help erect and then uphold such views as genuinely held.

CULTURAL ASSIMILATION, RACISM AND BAD SOCIAL GLUE

The subject of racism has been touched on in other parts of this book (Chapters 2 and 7), but it is worth considering here as another form of "bad belonging". Many countries around the world appear to be cohesive units with a strong sense of national identity, and this cohesion and the solidarity individuals feel towards one another can be likened to a strong sense of belonging. However, while local-born individuals may feel a strong sense of belonging to their country and each other, this may not transfer to foreigners, migrants or travellers, especially when these "others" retain their own sense of cultural identity.

Cultural assimilation happens when the minority groups or non-native residents of a country renounce their own culture, language and values and adopt instead the culture of the country in which they are residing. We see modern versions of this occurring all around the world, with migrants to new countries being asked to adopt the local language and cultural practices to show that they belong. More extreme examples can be found in relatively recent history. The practice of "Russification" during Stalin's reign, for instance, saw the loss of indigenous languages and the banning of them being taught in schools, in the name of national unity.

Indeed, even Hitler may have been chasing a sense of belonging in Germany before the Second World War. This is an uncomfortable thought, but it is important to consider just how far people will go in pursuit of a sense of belonging. The atrocities, ostracism and genocidal ideology of the 1930s and 1940s may well have been motivated in part by a desire to fulfil this fundamental human need. Kühne (2010) suggests that "through committing the Holocaust, Germans gained a feeling for a grand utopia of belonging" (p. 1). He adds that the killings and the destruction of "them" served to strengthen the love that was held between "us". During this period, the Germans were, he argues, acting more cohesively as a unit than they had done previously, and their desire for collective belonging was a motivating factor that led many individuals to kill as a symbol of brotherhood. Hatred and genocide can be seen, rather uncomfortably, as having provided a social glue for German society.

RIOTS

Riots can often emerge as an extension of racism and nationalism and within their own right offer a sense of bad belonging. In 2005, in the beachside suburb of Cronulla in Sydney, New South Wales, Australia experienced a bout of civil unrest between a group of men of Middle Eastern descent on the one side and white Anglo-Saxon lifeguards on the other. These events ultimately involved over 5,000 people and became known as the Cronulla riots. The Cronulla riots were a manifestation of Islamophobia, with rioters targeting those perceived as religiously or culturally Muslim in what was later described as an outbreak of "unbelonging". This sense of unbelonging is captured in an interview conducted by Itaoui and Dunn (2017) during their research into the events:

> Nah not Cronulla, never there. . . . No never, it's just a feeling I've got especially after the incident that happened there. . . . I haven't been there personally myself but I have developed this fear that if I go there, there will be something like you know, they definitely will do something wrong, so I won't go there . . . but yeah like Cronulla Beach I said that I, I've never been there but just because you know my community perceive it as a non-friendly beach for Muslims and Hijabis I avoid it, like I don't go there.
>
> (Woman, 28, Merrylands)

Unfortunately, the media reporting of the riot reinforced stereotypes and perceptions of otherness which contributed to the exclusion and unbelonging of the Muslim community. These effects were still being felt more than 15 years later. Sadly, it is unlikely that mindless mob behaviour that predicts riots. Research suggests that a strong sense of social identity can be responsible for shaping group norms and acceptance of collective violence.

Yet, as Riley (2020) suggests, we are all vulnerable to becoming outsiders. In fact, people are more displaced now than they have been in any other decade, due to displacement from war, famine, changes in weather patterns and climate change. In much of her work, Riley draws from the poetry of Benjamin Zephaniah, who emphasises that we are all, in fact, vulnerable to becoming refugees.

As identified by Benjamin Zephaniah in We Refugees, belonging can be impermanent. Society's attitudes can shift between othering and belonging; the "us" can quickly become the "them". We are all vulnerable to being outsiders.

THE GOOD, THE BAD AND THE BELONGING

During the completion of the manuscript for this book in 2020, COVID-19, a highly contagious respiratory illness, became a global pandemic. The speed at which the virus spread was a stark reminder of just how close we all are as a global community. Ironically, that very closeness made it necessary to take unprecedented measures aimed at social isolation and physical distancing (initially referred to as social distancing). Many countries closed their schools and universities, people worked from home, state and country borders were blocked and flights were cancelled. People were encouraged to stay home and banned from gathering in public places. These physical restrictions posed a barrier to belonging for many, and those who were already socially isolated, lonely and economically disadvantaged fared the worst. In the early weeks of the pandemic, we saw footage of empty supermarket shelves and abuse and brawls over necessities like toilet paper. It seemed that people were making individualistic choices on one hand while very much responding to collective anxiety on the other. Despite the chaos and the challenges posed by COVID-19, messages of connection were also shared. Some supermarkets began to open early for the elderly and healthcare workers, people took steps to look out for their neighbours and social media was used to share information on community support and resources. Stories of kindness and compassion emerged. One lady posted that she had seen a woman arrive at the checkout of her local supermarket wearing a facemask. She apologised to the cashier for the measures she had taken and explained that she had cancer and needed to protect herself. The cashier's response was to pull out her own credit card and pay for the woman's groceries. Neighbours shared dinners sitting at appropriate distances in their driveways; the elderly in aged care homes were visited by their children and grandchildren at their windows. Japan donated supplies to China in boxes bearing a Buddhist poem: "We have different mountains and rivers, but we share the same sun, moon and sky". The COVID-19 pandemic was an opportunity to see humans at their worst and at their best, but if anything, it highlighted our desire to connect with one another and our drive to find alternative ways to live our lives as social beings, despite the challenges before us. Social media, which has often been criticised for hindering belonging, triumphed in its ability to meaningfully connect people. Our need to belong was in the spotlight as many people felt the effects of isolation and distancing.

TOWARDS BUILDING BELONGING

As we have seen in this chapter, our human need to belong can push the limits of social norms. George Monbiot (2017), an environmental and political activist, argues that a new story is needed to overcome the many tensions in society that contribute to our questioning our sense of belonging, to create a fresh perspective for a society founded on kindness. Given that belonging and togetherness are inherent to us, he suggests that a community based on bridging networks where diverse groups of people can all feel a sense of belonging is needed. Chapter 7 examines how as an individual and as a community we can build belonging for our self and others.

7

BUILDING BELONGING

An ancient Chinese parable tells the story of an old man who knew he would die soon. Desiring to know what heaven and hell were like, he went to visit a wise man in his village: "Can you tell me what heaven and hell are like?" he asked. The wise man led him down a strange path that took them far out of the village and deep into the countryside. Finally, the pair came upon a large house with many rooms. Inside they found lots of people and many enormous tables set with an incredible array of food. Suddenly, the old man noticed a strange thing: the people, all thin and hungry despite the available food, were holding chopsticks 12 feet long. They tried to feed themselves, but they were unable to get the food to their mouths with such long chopsticks. The old man turned to the wise man and asked, "Now that I know what hell looks like, will you please show me what heaven looks like?" The wise man led him down the same path a little further until they came upon another large house like the first. Inside they found many people, all well fed and happy, and all carrying chopsticks 12 feet long. This puzzled the old man. "I see all of these people have 12-foot-long chopsticks as well, yet they are well fed and happy. Please explain this to me". The wise man replied, "In heaven, we feed each other" (Original source unknown). This parable reflects the core of what belonging is all about – it is about a willingness to belong together, to work together, to help each other, but also to have the skills to do all these things well.

Many branches of psychological research recognise a significant divide between the theoretical understanding of a particular area and application of that understanding in treatment, practice and intervention. In the case of belonging research, the field has benefited from decades of theoretical development and broad multidisciplinary input and from centuries of broader philosophical and sociological reflection on the relationship between the individual and the group. Perhaps because of the sheer scale and complexity of the work on the topic, a significant practice gap has opened.

While a gap between theory, research and practice is an important cause for concern, another issue emerges from the societal-level effects of a lack of belonging. Here we see a gap between theory, research and life – that is, a gap between how people can harness research to increase their own sense of belonging in their day-to-day experiences and interactions. Not everybody that experiences low belonging or loneliness will seek psychological help. Thus, if theoretical and research advances are to have an impact on as many individual lives as possible, we need to ensure that there is a foundational understanding at the community level of the importance of a sense of belonging for psychological and physical health. It is only once there is a widespread recognition of the importance of belonging that we can put in place the social structures to support those who might be the least likely to reach out for help by themselves. And it is only once there is a widespread focus on advancing abilities and skills relating to belonging that the tools will be available to maximise the benefits that can be offered.

Research is now well underway into the possibility of pharmaceutical approaches to treating loneliness (Cacioppo et al., 2014, 2015). However, a pill to "cure" the negative psychological consequences of loneliness may only further pathologise a common human condition. A pharmacological approach also risks bypassing psychotherapeutic and social interventions that are known to be effective and that can deliver the positive social effects of belonging, an outcome that will never be available in pill form, because these effects require an actual relationship between the individual and the group. Psychology has a lot to offer in responding to loneliness and a lack of belonging. The concluding chapter of this book aims to examine belonging as a construct that we can strengthen, nurture and develop, both in ourselves and in others, and it will reflect on research that can be applied to our everyday lives.

SOCIAL CONTAGION AND FINDING SIMILARITIES

Social contagion can be thought of as the passing on of behaviours from one person to another, usually in the same social network. Burgess and colleagues (2018) note that we tend to think about "social contagion" in the context of negative behaviours that can circulate through communities, such as suicide, poor body image, obesity, smoking, self-harm, school shootings and civil unrest. In fact, a much wider range of behaviours and thought patterns can be socially contagious. Some of these, such as yawning, are socially neutral, but many have strong positive connotations, as is the case with smiling or laughing. Similarly, behaviours that promote a culture of inclusion or belonging can also be contagious.

Social contagion normally takes place in a shared social network, and this may be one reason why members of friendship groups often share similarities. However, not all similarities between friends are a consequence of social contagion. On the contrary, people often become friends precisely because they share pre-existing perceived similarities. This tendency to come together with those who share similar interests is sometimes described as homophily (friendship towards the same). But while homophily may be a starting point for friendships, social contagion frequently works in a syncretic way, to draw friends even closer together by strengthening and adding similarities.

Kandel (1978) examined the effects of homophily (perceived similarity) on the different forms and stages of friendships among adolescents. Similarities in levels of educational aspirations, participation in minor delinquency, frequency of current marijuana use and political orientation were evaluated throughout friendships, from the establishment of the friendship to its dissolution. Kandel found that similarities between the two people predicted friendship development, but further similarities originated from the friendship as it developed as well. More recently, Gehlbach and colleagues (2016) carried out research into relationships guided by the assumption that when people see themselves as similar to someone else, they are more likely to like them as a result. In the study, students in an intervention group received feedback on five similarities they had with their teachers, while each teacher received feedback regarding their similarities with their students. The findings demonstrated both improved student–teacher relationships and higher course grades. It is feasible to assume that when people perceive similarities with others, they find it easier to build connections with them.

These results show that spending time getting to know one another can be a critical component in building belonging between groups and people and can serve as a powerful tool for breaking down barriers. Much research in this space has been conducted by Arthur Aron, who has spent decades developing the Fast Friends Intervention (sometimes referred to as 36 questions), to build interpersonal relationships and bonding (particularly between couples). This intervention works with pairs and small groups. The participants ask each other 36 questions split into three sets. These questions are not of the inconsequential type that is common in small talk but are framed instead to enable people to genuinely get to know one another quickly, effectively and, some might say, *deeply* (Aron et al., 1997).

Fast Friends

Time Required: 45 minutes each time you do this practice.

How to Do It

1 Identify someone with whom you'd like to become closer. It could be someone you know well or someone you're just getting to know. Although this exercise has a reputation for making people *fall in love*, it is actually useful for anyone you want to feel close to, including family members, friends, and acquaintances. Before

trying it, make sure both you and your partner are comfortable with sharing personal thoughts and feelings with each other.

2 Find a time when you and your partner have at least 45 minutes free and are able to meet in person.

3 For 15 minutes, take turns asking one another the questions in Set I below. Each person should answer each question, but in an alternating order, so that a different person goes first each time.

4 After 15 minutes, move on to Set II, even if you haven't yet finished the Set I questions. Then spend 15 minutes on Set II, following the same system.

5 After 15 minutes on Set II, spend 15 minutes on Set III. (Note: Each set of questions is designed to be more probing than the previous one. The 15-minute periods ensure that you spend an equivalent amount of time at each level of self-disclosure.)

SET I

1 Given the choice of anyone in the world, whom would you want as a dinner guest?

2 Would you like to be famous? In what way?

3 Before making a telephone call, do you ever rehearse what you are going to say? Why?

4 What would constitute a "perfect" day for you?

5 When did you last sing to yourself? To someone else?

6 If you were able to live to the age of 90 and retain either the mind or body of a 30-year-old for the last 60 years of your life, which would you want?

7 Do you have a secret hunch about how you will die?

8 Name three things you and your partner appear to have in common.

9 For what in your life do you feel most grateful?

10 If you could change anything about the way you were raised, what would it be?

11 Take four minutes and tell your partner your life story in as much detail as possible.

12 If you could wake up tomorrow having gained any one quality or ability, what would it be?

SET II

13 If a crystal ball could tell you the truth about yourself, your life, the future, or anything else, what would you want to know?

14 Is there something that you've dreamed of doing for a long time? Why haven't you done it?

15 What is the greatest accomplishment of your life?

16 What do you value most in a friendship?

17 What is your most treasured memory?

18 What is your most terrible memory?

19 If you knew that in one year you would die suddenly, would you change anything about the way you are now living? Why?

20 What does friendship mean to you?

21 What roles do love and affection play in your life?

22 Alternate sharing something you consider a positive characteristic of your partner. Share a total of five items.

23 How close and warm is your family? Do you feel your childhood was happier than most other people's?

24 How do you feel about your relationship with your mother?

SET III

25 Make three true "we" statements each. For instance, "We are both in this room feeling . . ."

26 Complete this sentence: "I wish I had someone with whom I could share . . ."

27 If you were going to become a close friend with your partner, please share what would be important for them to know.

28 Tell your partner what you like about them; be very honest this time, saying things that you might not say to someone you've just met.

29 Share with your partner an embarrassing moment in your life.

30 When did you last cry in front of another person? By yourself?

31 Tell your partner something that you like about them (already).

32 What, if anything, is too serious to be joked about?

33 If you were to die this evening with no opportunity to communicate with anyone, what would you most regret not having told someone? Why haven't you told them yet?

34 Your house, containing everything you own, catches fire. After saving your loved ones and pets, you have time to safely make a final dash to save any one item. What would it be? Why?

35 Of all the people in your family, whose death would you find most disturbing? Why?

36 Share a personal problem and ask your partner's advice on how they might handle it. Also, ask your partner to reflect back to you how you seem to be feeling about the problem you have chosen.

Source: Aron et al., 1997. Reprinted with permission

These questions were originally designed for couples to facilitate closeness and passionate love; however, the questions can be used to facilitate a sense of belonging between members of a group.

WHY DOES FAST FRIENDS WORK?

Attributing something to someone can be understood as the process of reaching conclusions based on the way a person is behaving (Heider, 1958). Attribution theory is used to explain how we perceive the nature and causes of other people's behaviour. Taking the time to get to know each other helps us to avoid fundamental attribution errors (i.e. to avoid drawing incorrect inferences about why people act as they do). These errors often involve concluding that the action of another is dispositional – a result of the person's disposition or character – when in fact it is not. Incorrect inferences about whether behaviour is dispositional can lead us to change the way we think about individuals, because we take the behaviour we observe as revealing something about the type of person they are. This approach to understanding others is extremely common – most of us are *dispositionalists* most of the time – but it also frequently leads us into error. People often behave in a given way due to long- or short-term environmental factors, personal beliefs or personal histories about which we may not be aware. For instance, someone might seem cold or rude towards a work colleague, and this might lead me to conclude that they are a cold or rude person. However, their behaviour may be the consequence of a number of reasons – a bad breakup, stress caused by facing financial difficulties, the loss of a friend or other specific psychological stressors. Failing to take the possibility of such non-dispositional factors into account will lead to the formation of an inaccurate view of the person.

Attribution theory attempts to take such factors into account in analysing and understanding behaviour. During the COVID-19 pandemic of 2020, shop shelves were sometimes stripped of essential products like toilet paper and hand sanitiser due to panic buying. As a result, fights sometimes occurred as customers competed for the items that they thought they needed. According to one viral story, a lady observed a man walking through a supermarket pushing a trolley filled to the brim with toilet paper and hand sanitiser in vast quantities. Furious, the lady approached the man and unloaded a barrage of insults at him, castigating him for being selfish, greedy and thoughtless, not to mention a danger to his fellow citizens. Once the tirade was over, the man politely responded: "I just work here ma'am. If you would kindly step out of the way, I need to keep on stocking the shelves." Apocryphal as this story may be, it illustrates the kind of snap conclusions we can come to about who people are and why they act when we do not actually have enough information to come to accurate conclusions. Fast Friends works because it pushes our understanding of the other past the level of making poorly grounded dispositional assumptions. Instead, it allows us to take the time to genuinely get to know other people.

PERCEPTIONS OF BELONGING

This single-item measure (Figure 7.1) was developed by Arthur Aron and colleagues (1992) to evaluate how close the respondent feels with another person or group, but it can be used equally well

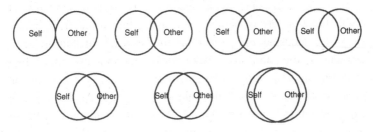

Figure 7.1 Aron and colleagues' (1992) inclusion of the other in the self scale.

for measuring a sense of belonging. Think of a group to which you belong, and consider the circles in Figure 7.1 with that group in mind. Which one of the circles best represents your sense of belonging to your group? Have there been times when you have identified with another pair of circles? Think about other groups you belong to. How does your belonging look for different groups when you compare them to each other?

Belonging is subjective because it is based on our perceptions at any given moment. A great deal of research has focused on addressing the cognitions, stereotypes and attribution errors that can contribute to a low sense of belonging to others (Mello et al., 2012; Yeager & Walton, 2011).

When cognitions arise that relate to outgroups or negative events caused by others, certain beliefs can create a buffer against the feeling of not belonging (Baumeister et al., 2007). Those individuals who understand that people can change and, thus, recognise that they themselves can change too are able to see that feelings of not belonging are likely to be transient. Similarly, individuals who believe that humans are generally more similar than different are insulated from broad feelings of not belonging. These protective factors also have implications for how we create belonging for the people around us and how we feel a sense of fitting into the different contexts in which we live and work.

Researchers like Greg Walton are leading the way in how we understand and apply brief, psychologically *wise* interventions to address social issues such as belonging uncertainty. A growing body of work highlights a variety of significant changes that result from simple exercises, focusing on preventing fundamental attribution error. Drawing on the tradition of attributional retraining, the aim of these interventions (e.g. social belonging interventions) is to help people understand that feelings of not belonging can be normal, commonly experienced and easily overcome. Other interventions to increase belonging aim to challenge peoples' beliefs about others and allow them to see that other people are different and yet also more similar than they may think. This work seeks to shift cognitions around social inclusion and to create opportunities to belong for self and others (Aron et al., 1997).

SOCIAL SKILLS

Social skills and other social and emotional competencies are also important for fostering belonging (Allen et al., 2017, 2018; Baumeister et al., 2005). These foundational skills provide the basic interpersonal tools that allow individuals to relate to one another and to ensure that their behaviour is consistent with the social norms of a group, thus enabling them to belong. Skills related to emotional and behavioural regulation are also important in this context and especially for preventing social rejection as we saw in Chapter 4. A growing number of schools purposely teach and prioritise social and emotional skills, acknowledging the important preventative role they play for wellbeing (Allen et al., 2017, 2018).

While social skills help to orientate social connections, a desire to work together, to be with others and to belong to a group or groups is also necessary; that is, people need also to see the *value* in belonging to groups (Leary & Allen, 2011).

MOTIVATION TO BELONG

While many people purport to prefer their own company, we know that rejecting the company of others can often result in suffering and struggle. Various theories have been advanced to explain why motivation is a key requirement for belonging (Baumeister & Leary, 1995; Maner et al., 2007). The belongingness hypothesis of Baumeister and Leary (1995) is one of the most widely cited starting points for explorations of the subject. What underpins this hypothesis is the understanding that humans are born with a drive towards belonging and that the desire to belong to others can be as necessary as food and shelter. Leary and Allen (2011) suggest that belongingness motivation is accompanied by a desire for self-presentation in order to increase relational value. Most people want to be liked and accepted by others and as a result, people may be motivated to engage in interpersonal behaviours that demonstrate they are cooperative, competent or successful. It is possible that even the simple act of apologising or offering a helping hand may demonstrate belongingness motivation in someone (Leary & Allen, 2011).

Another theory that recognises the importance of motivation is self-determination theory (Ryan & Deci, 2000). This theory of motivation suggests that three psychological needs – competence, relatedness and autonomy – must be met to fulfil optimal motivation for people in any context (e.g., sport, school, work). We might even speculate that these needs are required for people to be motivated to belong to different groups as well.

OPPORTUNITIES TO BELONG

While motivation and skills are needed for belonging to occur, a vital component that is often overlooked, perhaps due to its simplicity, is opportunity. The need for opportunities to belong may seem obvious, but it is nevertheless an important component that can usefully be targeted by interventions aimed at addressing loneliness and a lack of belonging (Gere & MacDonald, 2010). Membership in schools, workplaces, extracurricular groups, church groups, families and friendship groups and participation in hobbies are just some examples of opportunities for the human connections that are required for a sense of belonging.

Our knowledge about the importance of opportunities for belonging has emerged from research that has observed and examined cases in which there is a lack of belonging. For instance, research that has studied people from rural or isolated areas, first- and second-generation migrants or people with refugee backgrounds who lack opportunities to belong has found that members of these groups have greater difficulty managing psychological wellbeing, physical health and transition (Correa-Velez et al., 2010; Keyes & Kane, 2004). For some people, opportunities for education, training and employment (e.g. Correa-Velez et al., 2010) are vital for feelings of belonging to occur. Likewise, in a school setting, school attendance can be a prerequisite for school belonging (Bowles & Scull, 2018).

In the absence of physical opportunities for belonging, technology, such as social media and online gaming, may be able to help meet this need. These avenues for belonging have been found to be especially viable for youths (Davis, 2012) and for those who are introverted or shy or who have social anxiety (Amichai-Hamburger et al., 2002; Moore & McElroy, 2012; Seidman, 2013).

The simple act of joining a group is not all that is needed for there to be a genuine opportunity to belong. At the same time, we need to be able to feel safe in the group, be accepted and respected and have a sense of meaning and purpose. When people report dissatisfaction with the groups to which they belong, they may question their belonging or seek belonging elsewhere. It is for this reason that we need to understand belonging *both* as a human experience *and* as something that can be developed and nurtured.

BUILDING INDIVIDUAL BELONGING

When do we need to work with psychologists to build a sense of belonging? Psychologists can play an important role in building an individual's understanding and knowledge of the importance of belonging in society. This role is fulfilled primarily through psychoeducation but also by teaching and training people to learn and understand the social and emotional competencies (including social skills) that underpin the ability to belong. Psychologists may work in schools and be responsible for designing and implementing curricula for teaching these skills. Alternatively, they may pursue these goals by working with groups or individuals to help foster a sense of belonging. One such application is family therapy.

FAMILY THERAPY

Mother Teresa (1979) once said "try to do something. First in our own home, next door neighbor in the country we live, in the whole world". Given the fundamental nature of the family unit to so much of human experience, it is perhaps unsurprising that one of the most important systems for building a sense of belonging starts with the family. Psychologists have sought to tackle issues of belonging from this direction for decades. The emergence of general systems theory in the 1950s drew the attention of many psychologists away from individuals as free-floating "points" and towards a more systemic view of *relationships* and relationship issues between individuals who are embedded in a network of social systems (Becvar & Becvar, 2000). One application of general systems theory is *family therapy*, where the family is considered to be key to an individual's healthy psychological functioning. Minuchin (1974) suggests that although it may be an issue of a specific individual that motivates the initial need for therapy, the symptoms identified may well be a product of, or be maintained by, the family system of which the individual is a part. After all, we are all connected to broader systems and much of our life is spent navigating our relationship with these systems. For example, an individual's presenting problem may turn out to be an expression of family dysfunction or an issue that has been sustained by interactions in the family.

INDIVIDUAL THERAPY

Most humans constantly evaluate whether they belong to or fit in with those around them; those who are unable to evaluate their sense of belonging or interpersonal relationships can struggle socially, often defaulting to a low sense of belonging. Psychologists use a range of interventions and strategies to increase a sense of belonging, such as cognitive behaviour therapy, rational emotive behaviour therapy, solution-focused therapy, narrative therapy and acceptance commitment therapy (to name a few). Many of these strategies focus on investigating the thoughts, feelings and behaviours that underpin feelings of not belonging and on harnessing strategies that support perceptions of belonging and encourage solution-focused outcomes that improve the belonging experience of the client. For example, a psychologist may work with a client who reports that "my friends hate me", that they "always ignore me" and that "I don't belong here". These thoughts represent internal beliefs that shape a person's feelings and, ultimately, their behaviour. Beliefs and feelings of this sort can be responsible for a person's withdrawing from a friendship circle and investing little effort in relationships because of the disconfirming messages they are amplifying. A psychologist may spend time analysing the automatic thoughts associated with not feeling a sense of belonging and then provide ways that the client can challenge and overcome these thoughts to acquire a more rationally grounded perspective on their current state of belonging.

NOSTALGIA

The use of nostalgia has also been explored to foster a sense of belonging. Nostalgia originates from the Ancient Greek words *nostos*, meaning home, and *algos*, meaning pain or sorrow. A study by Cuervo and Cook (2018) explored participants' experiences relating to relationships with the place in which they grew up. The researchers found that nostalgia had a role to play in participants' decisions to stay or move away from these places. The results of the study showed that nostalgia encouraged emotions associated with comfort and familiarity, which serve as protective factors against uncertainties stemming from rapid social change. It thus seems possible that nostalgia has the capacity to positively affect the present.

IS THERE A ROLE FOR OXYTOCIN IN BUILDING BELONGING?

If oxytocin had an Instagram account, it would be a leading influencer. But just like those with large followings online, oxytocin does not always influence people for all the right reasons.

Oxytocin is a hormone that plays an important role in processes of bonding between people and groups. Endocrinological research has demonstrated the importance of oxytocin – sometimes known as the herding hormone – in social inclusion and social bonding, providing strong evidence that it motivates ingroup cooperation. In particular, several studies have shown a strong link between oxytocin and powerful prosocial effects, such as cooperation, trust, empathy, social bonding (Fujii et al., 2016) and compliance with group norms and cultural practices (De Dreu & Kret, 2016). There are good reasons, then, to think that oxytocin is a key player on the biological side of belonging.

Nevertheless, we should be wary about seeing it as some kind of silver bullet and assuming that the association between oxytocin and group activity offers us an unproblematic path towards fostering belonging. Much of the research demonstrating the benefits of oxytocin and its effects on cooperation, trust, ethnocentrism, conformity, empathy and favouritism tends to associate its effects with ingroup members only. These results have led to speculation that the hormone may also be related to racism, social categorisation and negative judgements of others. The reality is that many factors can influence prosocial behaviours, and the role that oxytocin plays in this matrix has yet to be fully understood. What we do know is that attachment and belonging are not controlled by oxytocin alone.

COMMUNITY BELONGING

In 2018, the UK included loneliness for the first time as part of a ministerial-level portfolio. Around the same time, a Campaign to End Loneliness also emerged in the UK, and activists in Australia formed the Australian Coalition to End Loneliness (ACEL). The concerning global spike in loneliness has since pushed the issue to the forefront of government attention all around the world. Alongside the increasing volume of debate around how best to tackle loneliness, concerns were also raised by some about loneliness – a normal, commonly occurring human emotion – being pathologised. This is despite the fact that many of the most important messages around belonging and inclusion already circulate at the community level, and there are many community groups, campaigns and events around the world that build belonging that perhaps require more attention.

ACT-BELONG-COMMIT

The Act-Belong-Commit campaign emerged from Western Australia over a decade ago and has since crossed the seas to take root more recently in Denmark. Act-Belong-Commit is a population-wide mental health promotion campaign. Belonging is one of the key factors that it targets in pursuit of this goal. The basic tenets of the campaign are to encourage people to do the following:

- Be physically and mentally active
- Belong to groups
- Commit to things with a greater meaning and purpose.

The campaign targets individuals with the goal of encouraging them to engage in activities that are both proactive and preventive, towards developing mental health problems. Importantly, the health promotion campaign has received empirical support through research (Donovan et al., 2006).

The campaign is unique in that it targets multiple communities, raises awareness through social marketing and seeks to improve community-level understanding of what it means to be active, have a sense of belonging and commit to activities. Similar campaigns have seen high levels of success targeting sunscreen use, obesity and smoking. This approach to mental health not only reduces stigma but also equips individuals with proactive and preventive tools that they can use to help themselves.

THE KITCHENER AND WATERLOO COMMUNITY FOUNDATION

The project Belonging Is was the product of a community management assessment conducted by the Kitchener and Waterloo Community Foundation (KWCF). Belonging Is was created to develop a useful model that would investigate and enhance the current state of belonging in the Kitchener, Waterloo and Woolwich communities. A total of 160 residents participated in the project and identified their feelings associated with belongingness, including being safe, content, happy, supported, relaxed, accepted and valued. The facilitation of these feelings became key goals for the community in order to support and enhance a sense of belonging among members.

I AM TRIANGLE

In 2013, in an effort to build social relationships and community connectedness, Naomi Hattaway, a global community leader and director of Habitat for Humanity of Omaha, founded I Am Triangle, a home for a global community where everyone belongs. I Am Triangle is an online platform that enables anyone from any part of the world to interact and communicate with other people. Finding common interests and appreciation for the presence and participation of others creates an opportunity for belongingness. At the same time, it also generates pathways for coping with loneliness, depression and stressful situations by encouraging social acceptance and building community connectedness.

EUROVISION

This chapter has focused primarily on steps that can be taken deliberately to build a sense of belonging, but sometimes events that may have been created for an entirely different purpose can build belonging unintentionally. The Eurovision Song Contest provides an example of this phenomenon. This multinational event with a 60-year history has become a major source of belonging for the LGBTIQ+ community. It is sometimes now even referred to as the Gay Olympics or the Gay World Cup and has become a meaningful space for members of the LGBTIQ+ community, particularly those who come from participating countries where conservative – even oppressive – attitudes and laws prevail regarding same-sex relationships and gender diversity.

In most parts of the world, a history of discrimination has defined the LGBTIQ+ community. For many people, Eurovision has provided a sense of solace from some of the negative experiences of the LGBTIQ+ community. At the same time, it offers a fascinating case study for the examination of belonging. The reason the event is such a rich object of study is that belonging is achieved and supported through multiple mechanisms:

1 **Eurovision has driven political change.** While it is commonly understood that Eurovision is apolitical, the thematic content of the songs have a history of advocating togetherness and belonging, such as "Together" (2016), "We Are One" (2013), "Celebrate Diversity" (2017) and "All Aboard" (2018). The positive endorsement of the rainbow flag has also been a feature of many of the contests, possibly most overtly when Eurovision was hosted by Ukraine and the organisers painted the historic *Peoples' Friendship Arch* – symbolising the friendship between Russia and Ukraine – in rainbow colours. This kind of support for often-marginalised groups has led some scholars to argue that Eurovision has played a role in influencing the views of national leaders and contributing to political change.

2 **Eurovision provides representation and visibility.** The fact that Eurovision serves as a stage for the visibility and representation of sexual and gender diversity (as far back as the 1990s) is perhaps the most significant reason for the contest's importance to the LGBTIQ+ community. When Greg Walton discusses his highly

successful social belonging intervention, one of the most important factors that he identifies for increasing a sense of belonging in participants is the visible representation of minority groups. An example of such representation at Eurovision can be seen in the 2013 performance of Ireland's Ryan O'Shaughnessy, who sang about love and struggle in romantic relationships while two male dancers depicted the relationships alongside him on stage. Similarly, when Conchita Wurst won the contest as a bearded drag queen the following year, the victory provided a global platform for those who departed from the societal norms of gender identity. Through the Eurovision contest, young people have opportunities to observe the safe self-expression of people who are less well represented on mainstream media platforms.

3 **Music is a source of belonging.** We also know that music has a role in supporting belonging in its own right. Many groups around the world have shown the value of songs in fostering group bonding and unity. Examples include the songs chirped by Danish school children at the start of each school day, the use of call-and-response songs or marching music in the military, the role played by anthems in the shaping of national identity, the bonds reaffirmed among friends while singing "Auld Lang Syne" to welcome a New Year, or songs used in religious settings. We also know that singing can make us feel good – the secretion of endorphins and oxytocin are among the neurochemical results of singing together with other people.

4 **Togetherness and community building are important.** Togetherness is a frequent, major theme of Eurovision. People come together for Eurovision at concert venues, in loungerooms and on social media. For some, the event provides an opportunity to meet others and gain access to LGBTIQ+ communities. In this way, it could be said that Eurovision serves the functions of building community and creating opportunities to bond with these groups, thus helping to create a social identity for members.

Eurovision offers a new and positive lens through which to view how belonging can be fostered at a community, and perhaps a global, level.

COMMUNITY SPORT AND BELONGING

While research points to a long-term decline in sport participation in both children and adults, recent studies have identified it as playing an important role in community- and personal-belonging. Most people who engage in team sports also value the benefits of teamwork and collaboration, an attitude that has been found to support belonging. Sports fandom can offer a sense of meaning and purpose in life for many members of the community. For refugee students, for example, sport provides an opportunity to meet others and build community.

TWO SIDES TO SPORT

However, sport has not always offered a place of belonging that is open to everybody. Even in recent history, some sports have seen instances of racial abuse that send disconfirming messages to both players and spectators. Mauro (2016) has emphasised how football (soccer) can act as a cause of discrimination and exclusion. For instance, in the Republic of Ireland, where football is a form of identification in the local community, Black male immigrants have faced a range of cultural barriers concerned with representation and racism that challenge their sense of belonging to and social inclusion in teams.

The Australian Football League (AFL) offers another example of sport's failure to offer a sense of belonging. Adam Goodes, an Indigenous Australian player, experienced racial vilification in 2013 after being called an "ape" by a spectator. He identified the offender – a 13-year-old girl – who was removed from the stadium by security. The following day, Goodes deflected blame from the teenager, claiming that she was most likely mirroring behaviour learned from her role models. Nevertheless, an insidious backlash against Goodes followed, and he was booed by large sections of spectators at subsequent matches, driving him to early retirement.

Goodes' actions and his other outspoken comments against racism turned some of the football community against him. At its heart, sport offers immense opportunities for social participation and belonging.

However, these stories illustrate that it does not exist outside of the broader issues in society that negatively affect belonging for certain people and groups. There remains much work to be done to ensure that all of sport's participants have equal opportunities to belong. Naturally, this work must extend to society more broadly to tackle issues of cultural insensitivity and racism.

Every member of society can be an advocate for inclusive behaviours and language. Belonging can be viewed through an inclusive lens that recognises the diversity of our global community – past and present. Our behaviours should not intentionally exclude members of a particular audience. On the contrary, they should actively seek to include and connect people. This means striving for consistently inclusive practices that preclude feelings of otherness. Schools, workplaces, communities and organisations must ensure that policy and practice are articulated in a way that fosters belonging and offers opportunities to belong and that the belonging message includes everyone.

A shared sense of belonging may lead to shared solutions for shared problems. One such shared problem is climate change. In this final section of the book, we'll touch on how a sense of belonging to the planet may offer a hopeful opportunity for change.

GLOBAL BELONGING

Climate change, or rather the *climate emergency* that we now face, has created unprecedented challenges for belonging. We are currently seeing the first waves of a demographic displacement of vast numbers of people spurred on to leave their homes behind by the pressures of climate change events such as severe weather patterns, droughts and wildfires. While not all people are willing to act on climate change science, the science itself is clear on one key point: climate change is very much a human-induced process, and it requires a human-induced response to tackle it. When we think about belonging to our planet and about how we should treat it, we might speculate that people who have a high sense of belonging to earth are more likely to engage in behaviours that respond in a positive way to climate change.

Place identity and *place attachment* are two concepts that are critically significant in the context of climate change and the human-environment relationship. Research suggests that when someone identifies themselves as belonging to the environment in which they live, they are more likely to engage in environmentally sustainable behaviours (Uzzell et al., 2002). Place identity refers to a sense of self that emerges from a specific place or physical environment, while place attachment describes the emotional attachment between a person and place (Swim et al., 2011). Although climate change is one of the most crucial issues of our time (Ferguson & Branscombe, 2010), it is easy for people to ignore the unfolding process due to it not having an immediate impact on them. A person's identification and attachment with a place may explain the type of bond they have with the environment. A weak bond, or lack of belonging to the environment, for instance, may be contributing to behaviours that lead to environmental deterioration. Our sense of belonging to the environment may also directly impact on how we perceive climate change efforts. A recent study found that people who have a stronger global connection with the environment are more likely to see the positive economic impacts that result from climate change responses in comparison to people with stronger national, as opposed to global, attachment (Devine-Wright et al., 2015). Many scholars have speculated that the human behavioural contributions to climate change are growing despite the increase in public awareness over climate change issues and responses. As bell hooks (2009) writes, "If we think of the natural landscapes that surround us as simply blank slates, existing for humans to act upon them according to our will then we cannot exist in life sustaining harmony with the earth" (p. 26). While further empirical evidence is needed to advance this field of research, it may be possible that approaches that encourage people's sense of belonging to the environment could contribute another perspective to existing climate change solutions.

OUR COMMON RACE IS THE HUMAN RACE

Belonging is essential for our psychological and physical health and can play a role in the way we think and interact with the world. The way we engage with others is central to our humanity. When feelings of *not belonging* arise, we have recourse to scientific literature that points us to practices that can counter such feelings.

A sense of belonging in childhood and adolescence is fundamental to the way we function throughout our lives. Therefore, proactive strategies are recommended, beginning from birth but with an emphasis on early childhood, when children first begin interacting with groups outside the family. Emphasising the importance of social skills and social and emotional competencies should be part of an ongoing curriculum in schools. We should also remember that *everybody* has the potential to create opportunities for belonging for others through our work, school and more common daily personal interactions.

We need to invest in belonging and to make it a priority – as a society, financially and through legislation. Belonging is intrinsic to the health, happiness and wellbeing of all people. While there are many differences between us, there are many more similarities. Despite our distinctions, we share a common need to belong. This collective need calls for a collective understanding that no matter how we choose to live our lives, belonging is core to so much of what we do. To rephrase the words of Morrissey from the Smiths in the song "How Soon is Now", "I am human and I need to be(long). Just everybody else does".

REFERENCES

CHAPTER 1

Ainsworth, M. D. S., & Bell, S. M. (1970). Attachment, exploration, and separation: Illustrated by the behavior of one-year-olds in a strange situation. *Child Development*, 41(1), 49–67.

Allen, K. A., Kern, M. L., Vella-Brodrick, D., Waters, L., & Hattie, J. (2018). What schools need to know about belonging: A meta-analysis. *Educational Psychology Review*, 30(1), 1–34. Retrieved from: https://doi.org/10.1007/s10648-016-9389-8

Allen, K. A., Vella-Brodrick, D., & Waters, L. (2016). Fostering school belonging in secondary schools using a socio-ecological framework. *The Educational and Developmental Psychologist*, 33(1), 97–121.

Allen, K. A., Vella-Brodrick, D., & Waters, L. (2018). Rethinking school belonging: A socio-ecological framework. In K. A. Allen & C. Boyle (Eds.), *Pathways to belonging: Contemporary research in school belonging* (1st ed., pp. 191–218). The Netherlands: Brill. Retrieved from: https://doi.org/10.1163/9789004386969_011

Baumeister, R. F., & Leary, M. R. (1995). The need to belong: Desire for interpersonal attachments as a fundamental human motivation. *Psychological Bulletin*, 11, 497-529.

Bowlby, J. (1988). Developmental psychiatry comes of age. *The American Journal of Psychiatry*, 145(1), 1-10. Retrieved from: https://doi.org/10.1176/ajp.145.1.1

Bronfenbrenner, U. (1979). *The ecology of human development: Experiments by nature and design.* Cambridge, MA: Harvard University Press.

Brown, B. (2010). *The gifts of imperfection: Let go of who you think you're supposed to be and embrace who you are.* Center City, MN: Hazelden.

Centers for Disease Control and Prevention. (2009). *School connectedness: Strategies for increasing protective factors among youth.* Atlanta, GA: U.S. Department of Health and Human Services.

Cortina, K. S., Arel, S., & Smith-Darden, J. P. (2017). School belonging in different cultures: The effects of individualism and power distance. *Frontiers in Educations*, 2, 1-11. Retrieved from: https://doi.org/10.3389/feduc.2017.00056

Glasser, W. (1986). *Control theory in the classroom.* New York, NY: Perennial Library/Harper & Row.

Gray, D. L., Yough, M., & Williams, W. A. (2019). My class needs my voice: The desire to stand out predicts choices to contribute during class discussions. *Educational & Child Psychology*, 36(4), 65–78.

Grove, C., & Henderson, L. (2018). Therapy dogs can help reduce student stress, anxiety and improve school attendance. *The Conversation.* https://theconversation.com/therapy-dogs-can-help-reduce-student-stress-anxiety-and-improve-school-attendance-93073

Hagerty, B. M., & Patusky, K. (1995). Developing a measure of sense of belonging. *Nursing Research*, 44(1), 9–13.

Leary, M. R. (2010). Affiliation, acceptance, and belonging: The pursuit of interpersonal connection. In S. T. Fiske, D. T. Gilbert, & G. Lindzey (Eds.), *Handbook of social psychology* (pp. 864–897). Hoboken, NJ: John Wiley & Sons Inc.

Leary, M. R., Tambor, E. S., Terdal, S. K., & Downs, D. L. (1995). Self-esteem as an interpersonal monitor: The sociometer hypothesis. *Journal of Personality and Social Psychology*, 68(3), 518–530. Retrieved from: https://doi.org/10.1037/0022-3514.68.3.518

Leerkes, E. M. (2011). Maternal sensitivity during distressing tasks: A unique predictor of attachment security. *Infant Behavior and Development*, 34(3), 443-446.

Maslow, A. H. (1968). *Toward a psychology of being.* New York, NY: D. Van Nostrand.

Maslow, A. H. (1971). *The farther reaches of human nature.* New York, NY: The Viking Press.

Masserman, J. H., Wechkin, S., & Terris, W. (1964). "Altruistic" behavior in rhesus monkeys. *American Journal of Psychiatry*, 121(6), 584–585.

Peterson, C. (2006). *A primer in positive psychology.* New York, NY: Oxford University Press.

Rogers, C. R. (1951). *Client-centered therapy; its current practice, implications, and theory.* Boston, MA: Houghton Mifflin.

Tomasello, M. (2014). The ultra-social animal. *European Journal of Social Psychology,* 44(3), 187–194.

Turner, T. (2017). *Remembering ourselves home.* Her Own Room Press, Salt Spring Island, British Columbia.

Von Bertalanffy, L. (1968). *Organismic psychology and systems theory (Vol. 1).* Worcester, MA: Clark University Press.

CHAPTER 2

Abdollahi, A., Panahipour, S., Tafti, M. A., & Allen, K. A. (2020). Academic hardiness as a mediator for the relationship between school belonging and academic stress. *Psychology in the Schools.* Retrieved from: https://doi.org/10.1002/pits.22339

Allen, K. A., & Boyle, B. (Eds.) (2016). Pathways to belonging. Editorial for the special issue on school belonging. *Educational and Developmental Psychologist,* 33(1), 1–21. Retrieved from: http://dx.doi.org/10.1017/edp.2016.5

Allen, K. A., Boyle, C., & Roffey, S. (2019). Creating a culture of belonging in a school context. Educational and child psychology, special issue on school belonging. *Educational and Child Psychology,* 36(4), 5–7.

Allen, K. A., & Kern, M. L. (2017). *School belonging in adolescents: Theory, research, and practice.* Singapore: Springer Social Sciences. ISBN 978-981-10-5996-4

Allen, K. A., Kern, M. L., Vella-Brodrick, D., Hattie, J., & Waters, L. (2018). What schools need to know about fostering school belonging: A meta-analysis. *Educational Psychology Review,* 30(1), 1–34. Retrieved from: https://doi.org/10.1007/s10648-016-9389-8

Allen, K. A., & Kern, P. (2019). *Boosting school belonging in adolescents: Interventions for teachers and mental health professionals.* Abingdon, UK: Routledge.

Allen, K. A., Ryan, T., Gray, D. L., McInerney, D. M., & Waters, L. (2014). Social media use and social connectedness in adolescents: The positives and the potential pitfalls. *The Educational and Developmental Psychologist,* 31(1), 18–31.

Allen, K. A., Vella-Brodrick, D., & Waters, L. (2017). School belonging and the role of social and emotional competencies in fostering an adolescent's sense of connectedness to their school. In E. Frydenberg, A. J. Martin, & R. J. Collie (Eds.), *Social and emotional learning in Australia and the Asia-Pacific: Perspectives, programs and approaches* (1st ed., pp. 83–99). Singapore: Springer. Retrieved from: https://doi.org/10.1007/978-981-10-3394-0_5

Arain, M., Haque, M., Johal, L., Mathur, P., Nel, W., Rais, A., Sandhu, R., & Sharma, S. (2013). Maturation of the adolescent brain. *Neuropsychiatric Disease and Treatment*, 9, 449–461.

Arslan, G., Allen, K. A., & Ryan, T. (2020). Exploring the impacts of school belonging on youth wellbeing and mental health: A longitudinal study. *Child Indicators Research*. Retrieved from: https://doi.org/10.1007/s12187-020-09721-z

Baron-Cohen, S., Leslie, A. M., & Frith, U. (1985). Does the autistic child have a "theory of mind"? *Cognition*, 21, 37–46.

Braddock, J. H., & Gonzalez, A. (2010). Social isolation and social cohesion: The effects of K-12 neighborhood and school segregation on intergroup orientations. *Teachers College Record*, 112, 1631–1653.

Burnett, S., Sebastian, C., Kadosh, K. C., & Blakemore, S. J. (2011). The social brain in adolescence: Evidence from functional magnetic resonance imaging and behavioural studies. *Neuroscience & Biobehavioral Reviews*, 35(8), 1654–1664.

Engelmann, J. M., Herrmann, E., & Tomasello, M. (2012). Five-year olds, but not chimpanzees, attempt to manage their reputations. *PLoS One*, 7(10), e48433. Retrieved from: https://doi.org/10.1371/journal.pone.0048433

Erikson, E. H. (1950). *Childhood and society.* New York: Norton.

Friedman, R. L. (2007). Widening the therapeutic lens: Sense of belonging as an integral dimension of the human experience. *Dissertation Abstracts International: Section B: Sciences and Engineering*, 68(5-B), 3394.

Fromkin, V., Krashen, S., Curtiss, S., Rigler, D., & Rigler, M. (1974). The development of language in Genie: A case of language acquisition beyond the 'critical period'. *Brain and Language*, 1, 81–107.

Frydenberg, E., Deans, J., & O'Brien, K. A. (2012). *Developing children's coping in the early years: Strategies for dealing with stress, change and anxiety.* London, UK: Bloomsbury. ISBN: 9781441161048

Gehlbach, H., Brinkworth, M. E., King, A. M., Hsu, L. M., McIntyre, J., & Rogers, T. (2016). Creating birds of similar feathers: Leveraging similarity to improve teacher–student relationships and academic achievement. *Journal of Educational Psychology*, 108(3), 342–352. Retrieved from: https://doi.org/10.1037/edu0000042

Gerlach, R., & Gockel, C. (2018). We belong together: Belonging to the principal's in-group protects teachers from the negative effects of task conflict on psychological safety. *School Leadership & Management*, 38(3), 302–322.

Gray, D. L., Hope, E. C., & Matthews, J. S. (2018). Black and belonging at school: A case for interpersonal, instructional, and institutional opportunity structures. *Educational Psychologist*, 53(2), 97–113.

Harrist, A. W., & Bradley, K. D. (2003). "You can't say you can't play": Intervening in the process of social exclusion in the kindergarten classroom. *Early Childhood Research Quarterly*, 18(2), 185–205.

Hattie, J. A. (2002). Classroom composition and peer effects. *International Journal of Educational Research*, 37(5), 449–481.

Haun, D. B., & Tomasello, M. (2011). Conformity to peer pressure in preschool children. *Child Development*, 82(6), 1759–1767.

Lenzi, M., Sharkey, J. D., Wroblewski, A., Furlong, M. J., & Santinello, M. (2019). Protecting youth from gang membership: Individual and school-level emotional competence. *Journal of Community Psychology*, 47(3), 563–578.

Lieberman, M. D. (2013). *Social: Why our brains are wired to connect*. New York, NY: Crown.

Ludy-Dobson, C. R., & Perry, B. D. (2010). The role of healthy relational interactions in buffering the impact of childhood trauma. In E. Gil (Ed.), *Working with children to heal interpersonal trauma: The power of play* (pp. 26–43). New York, NY: The Guilford Press.

Matthews, T., Danese, A., Wertz, J., Odgers, C. L., Ambler, A., Moffitt, T. E., & Arseneault, L. (2016). Social isolation, loneliness and depression in young adulthood: A behavioural genetic analysis. *Social Psychiatry and Psychiatric Epidemiology*, 51(3), 339–348. Retrieved from: https://doi.org/10.1007/s00127-016-1178-7

McMahon, S. D., Singh, J. A., Garner, L. S., & Benhorin, S. (2004). Taking advantage of opportunities: Community involvement, wellbeing, and urban youth. *Journal of Adolescent Health*, 34, 262–265.

Mensah, F. K., Bayer, J. K., Wake, M., Carlin, J. B., Allen, N. B., & Patton, G. C. (2013). Early puberty and childhood social and behavioral adjustment. *Journal of Adolescent Health*, 53(1), 118–124.

Okonofua, J. A., Paunesku, D., & Walton, G. M. (2016, May). Brief intervention cuts suspension rates in half. *Proceedings of the National Academy of Sciences May 2016*, 113(19), 5221–5226. Retrieved from: https://doi.org/10.1073/pnas.1523698113

Organisation for Economic Co-operation and Development (OECD). (2017). *PISA 2015 results (Volume III)*. Retrieved from: https://read.oecd-ilibrary.org/education/pisa-2015-results-volume-iii_9789264273856-en#page121

Osterman, K. F. (2000). Students' need for belonging in the school community. *Review of Educational Research, 70*(3), 323–367.

Over, H. (2016). The origins of belonging: Social motivation in infants and young children. *Philosophical Transactions of the Royal Society B: Biological Sciences, 371*(1686), 20150072. Retrieved from: http://dx.doi.org/10.1098/rstb.2015.0072

Pittman, L. D., & Richmond, A. (2007). Academic and psychological functioning in late adolescence: The importance of school belonging. *Journal of Experimental Education, 75*, 275–290.

Quinn, S., & Oldmeadow, J. A. (2013). Is the igeneration a 'we' generation? Social networking use among 9- to 13-year-olds and belonging. *British Journal of Developmental Psychology, 31*(1), 136–142.

Riley, K. (2020, January). *How to create schools which are places of welcome and belonging for all*. Keynote presented at the 33rd International Congress for School Effectiveness and Improvement (ICSEI). Marrakesh, Morocco.

Roffey, S., & Boyle, C. (2018). Belief, belonging and the role of schools in reducing the risk of home-grown extremism. In K. A. Allen & C. Boyle (Eds.), *Pathways to belonging: Contemporary research in school belonging* (pp. 149–164). The Netherlands: Brill Sense.

Roffey, S., Boyle, C., & Allen, K. A. (2019). School belonging – Why are our students longing to belong to school? *Educational and Child Psychology, 36*(2), 6–8.

Sapolsky, R. M. (2017). *Behave: The biology of humans at our best and worst*. New York, NY: Penguin Random House.

Shochet, I. M., Dadds, M. R., Ham, D., & Montague, R. (2006). School connectedness is an underemphasized parameter in adolescent mental health: Results of a community prediction study. *Journal of Clinical Child and Adolescent Psychology, 35*(2), 170–179.

Slaten, C. D., Ferguson, J. K., Allen, K. A., Vella-Brodrick, D., & Waters, L. (2016). School belonging: A review of the history, current trends, and future directions. *The Educational and Developmental Psychologist, 33*(1), 1–15. Retrieved from: https://doi.org/10.1017/edp.2016.6

St. Amand, J., Girard, S., & Smith, J. (2017). Sense of belonging at school: Defining attributes, determinants, and sustaining strategies. *IAFOR Journal of Education, 5*(2), 105–119.

Tajfel, H., & Turner, J. (1979). An integrative theory of intergroup conflict. In W. Austin & S. Worchel (Eds.), *The social psychology of intergroup relations* (pp. 33–47). Monterey, CA: Brooks/Cole.

The Aspen Institute. (2019). *State of play trends and developments in youth sports.* Retrieved from: https://assets.aspeninstitute.org/content/uploads/2019/10/2019_SOP_National_Final.pdf

Uwah, C., McMahon, G., & Furlow, C. (2008). *School belonging, educational aspirations, and academic self-efficacy among African American male high school students: Implications for school counselors.* Professional School Counseling. Retrieved from: http://www.thefreelibrary.com/School+belonging,+educational+aspirations,+and+academic+self-efficacy. . .-a0180860878

Wallace, T. L., Ye, F., & Chhuon, V. (2012). Subdimensions of adolescent belonging in high school. *Applied Developmental Science*, 16, 122–139.

Walton, G. M. (2014). The new science of wise psychological interventions. *Current Directions in Psychological Science*, 23(1), 73–82.

Wang, Z., & Wang, L. (2015). The mind and heart of the social child: Developing the empathy and theory of mind scale. *Child Development Research.* http://www.hindawi.com/journals/cdr/2015/171304/.

Wike, T. L., & Fraser, M. W. (2009). School shootings: Making sense of the senseless. *Aggression and Violent Behavior*, 14(3), 162–169. Retrieved from: https://doi.org/ 10.1016/j.avb.2009.01.005

Wingspread declaration on school connections (2004). Wingspread declaration on school connections. *Journal of School Health*, 74 (7), 233–234.

Wyman, P. A., Pickering, T. A., Pisani, A. R., Rulison, K., Schmeelk-Cone, K., Hartley, C., Gould, M., Caine, E. D., LoMurray, M., Brown, C. H., & Valente, T. W. (2019). Peer-adult network structure and suicide attempts in 38 high schools: Implications for network-informed suicide prevention. *The Journal of Child Psychology and Psychiatry*, 60(10), 1065–1075. Retrieved from: https://doi.org/ 10.1111/jcpp.13102

CHAPTER 3

The Administration for Community Living's Administration on Aging. (2018). *2017 profile of older Americans.* ACL. Retrieved from: https://acl.gov/sites/default/files/Aging%20and%20Disability%20in%20America/2017OlderAmericansProfile.pdf

Allen, K. A. (2020). Commentary of Lim, M., Eres, R., Gleeson, J., Long, K., Penn, D., & Rodebaugh, T. (2019). A pilot digital intervention targeting loneliness in youth mental health. *Frontiers in Psychiatry*. Retrieved from: https://doi.org/10.3389/fpsyt.2019.00959

Anderson, S., Currie, C., & Copeland, J. (2016). Sedentary behavior among adults: The role of community belonging. *Preventive Medicine Reports, 4*, 238–241. Retrieved from: http://dx.doi.org/10.1016/j.pmedr.2016.06.014

Barry, C. M., Madsen, S. D., & DeGrace, A. (2016). Growing up with a little help from their friends in emerging adulthood. In J. J. Arnett (Ed.), *The Oxford handbook of emerging adulthood* (pp. 215–229). New York, NY: Oxford University Press.

Boden-Albala, B. M., Litwak, E., Elkind, M. S. V., Rundek, T., & Sacco, R. L. (2005). Social isolation and outcomes post stroke. *Neurology, 64*(11), 1888–1892.

Cacioppo, J. T., Hawkley, L. C., Norman, G. J., & Berntson, G. G. (2011). Social isolation. *Annals of the New York Academy of Sciences, 1231*(1), 17–22.

Camara, M., Bacigalupe, G., & Padilla, P. (2017). The role of social support in adolescents: Are you helping me or stressing me out? *International Journal of Adolescence and Youth, 22*(2), 123–136. Retrieved from: https://doi.org/10.1080/02673843.2013.875480

Chesler, J., McLaren, S., Klein, B., & Watson, S. (2015). The effects of playing Nintendo Wii on depression, sense of belonging and social support in Australian aged care residents: A protocol study of a mixed methods intervention trial. *BMC Geriatrics, 15*(1), 106. Retrieved from: https://doi.org/10.1186/s12877-015-0107-z

Cohen, S., & Janicki-Deverts, D. (2009). Can we improve our physical health by altering our social networks? *Perspectives on Psychological Science, 4*(4), 375–378.

Cruwys, T., Dingle, G., Haslam, S. A., Haslam, C., Jetten, J., & Morton, T. A. (2013). Social group memberships protect against future depression, alleviate depression symptoms and prevent depression relapse. *Social Science and Medicine, 98*, 179–186. Retrieved from: https://doi.org/10.1016/j.socscimed.2013.09.013

Haslam, C., Holme, A., Haslam, S. A., Iyer, A., Jetten, J., & Williams, W. H. (2008). Maintaining group memberships: Social identity continuity predicts well-being after stroke. *Neuropsychological Rehabilitation, 18*(5–6), 671–691.

Haslam, S. A., Jetten, J., Postmes, T., & Haslam, C. (2009). Social identity, health and well-being: An emerging agenda for applied psychology. *Applied Psychology, 58*(1), 1–23.

Holt-Lunstad, J., Smith, T. B., & Layton, J. B. (2010). Social relationships and mortality risk: A meta-analytic review. *PLoS Med*, 7(7), e1000316.

Jakubec, S., Olfert, M., Choi, L., Dawe, N., & Sheehan, D. (2019). Understanding belonging and community connection for seniors living in the suburbs. *Urban Planning*, 4(2), 43–52. Retrieved from: https://doi.org/10.17645/up.v4i2.1896

Jetten, J., Haslam, C., Haslam, S. A., & Branscombe, N. R. (2009). The social cure. *Scientific American Mind*, 20(5), 26–33.

Kim, B., Park, S., Bishop-Saucier, J., & Amorim. (2017). Community based services and depression from person-environment fit perspective: Focusing on functional impairments and living alone. *Journal of Gerontological Social Work*, 60, 270–285. Retrieved from: https://doi.org/10.1080/01634372.2017.1310166

Lin, P. Y., Grewal, N. S., Morin, C., Johnson, W. D., & Zak, P. J. (2013). Oxytocin increases the influence of public service advertisements. *PloS One*, 8(2), e56934. Retrieved from: https://doi.org/10.1371/journal.pone.0056934

McLaren, S. (2020). The relationship between living alone, sense of belonging, and depressive symptoms among older men: The moderating role of sexual orientation. *Aging & Mental Health*, 24(1), 103–109. Retrieved from: https://doi.org/10.1080/13607863.2018.1531373

McLaren, S., Turner, J., Gomez, R., McLachlan, A. J., & Gibbs, P. M. (2013). Housing type and depressive symptoms among older adults: A test of sense of belonging as a mediating and moderating variable. *Aging & Mental Health*, 17(8), 1023–1029.

Novotney, A. (2019). Social isolation: It could kill you. *Monitor in Psychology*, 50(5), 32.

O'Connor, M. (2010). Life beyond school: The role of school bonding in preparing adolescents for adulthood. *Independence*, 35(1), 24–28.

Peralta, L. G., & Moreno, E. S. (2019). Successful ageing in older persons belonging to the Aymara native community: Exploring the protective role of psychosocial resources. *Health Psychology and Behavioral Medicine*, 7(1), 396–412. Retrieved from: https://doi.org/10.1080/21642850.2019.1691558

Price, B. (2015). Approaches to counter loneliness and social isolation. *Nursing Older People*, 27(7), 31–39. Retrieved from: http://0-dx.doi.org.aupac.lib.athabascau.ca/10.7748/nop.27.7.31.e722

Putnam, R. D. (2000). *Bowling alone: The collapse and revival of American community*. New York, NY: Simon and Schuster.

Seeman, T. E. (1996). Social ties and health: The benefits of social integration. *Annals of Epidemiology, 6*(5), 442–451.

Theeke, L. A., Mallow, J., Gianni, C., Legg, K., & Glass, C. (2015). The experience of older women living with loneliness and chronic conditions in Appalachia. *Journal of Rural Mental Health, 39*(2), 61–72.

Vélez, C. E., Krause, E. D., McKinnon, A., Brunwasser, S. M., Freres, D. R., Abenavoli, R. M., & Gillham, J. E. (2016). Social support seeking and early adolescent depression and anxiety symptoms: The moderating role of rumination. *The Journal of Early Adolescence, 36*(8), 1118–1143. Retrieved from: https://doi.org/10.1177/0272431615594460

White Wreath Association Ltd. (2020). *Personal suicide stories*. Retrieved from: http://www.whitewreath.org.au/articles/personal-stories/

CHAPTER 4

Adler, N. E., & Snibbe, A. C. (2003). The role of psychosocial processes in explaining the gradient between socioeconomic status and health. *Current Directions in Psychological Science, 12*(4), 119–123.

Albano, G., Rowlands, K., Baciadonna, L., Coco, G. L., & Cardi, V. (2019). Interpersonal difficulties in obesity: A systematic review and meta-analysis to inform a rejection sensitivity-based model. *Neuroscience and Biobehavioral Reviews, 107*, 846–861. Retrieved from: https://doi.org/10.1016/j.neubiorev.2019.09.039

Alexander, B. K., Coambs, R. B., & Hadaway, P. F. (1978). The effect of housing and gender on morphine self-administration in rats. *Psychopharmacology, 58*(2), 175–179.

Alexander, B. K., Peele, S., Hadaway, P. F., Morse, S. J., Brodsky, A., & Beyerstein, B. L. (1985). Adult, infant, and animal addiction. In S. Peele (Ed.), *The meaning of addiction* (pp. 77–96). Lanham, MD: Lexington Books.

Arrigo, B. A., & Bullock, J. L. (2008). The psychological effects of solitary confinement on prisoners in supermax units: Reviewing what we know and recommending what should change. *International Journal of Offender Therapy and Comparative Criminology, 52*(6), 622–640.

Badaly, D., Schwartz, D., & Gorman, A. H. (2012). Social status, perceived social reputations, and perceived dyadic relationships in early adolescence. *Social Development, 21*(3), 482–500.

Bogart, K. R., Lund, E. M., & Rottenstein, A. (2018). Disability pride protects self-esteem through the rejection-identification model. *Rehabilitation Psychology*, 63(1), 155–159.

Broomhead, K. E. (2019). Acceptance or rejection? The social experiences of children with special educational needs and disabilities within a mainstream primary school. *Education 3–13*, 47(8), 877–888.

Ciuhan, G. (2018). The feeling of rejection and humiliation and the avoidance of harm as predictors for aggressive behaviour in school-aged children in Romania. *European Journal of Special Needs Education*, 34(4), 530–537.

Eisenberger, N. I., Lieberman, M. D., & Williams, K. D. (2003). Does rejection hurt? An fMRI study of social exclusion. *Science*, 302(5643), 290–292.

Felix, S., Portugal, P., & Tavares, A. (2017). *Going after the addiction, not the addicted: The impact of drug decriminalization in Portugal*. IZA Institute of Labor Economics, Discussion Paper No. 10895.

Harrist, A. W., & Bradley, K. D. (2002). Social exclusion in the classroom: Teachers and students as agents of change. In J. Aronson (Ed.), *Improving academic achievement* (pp. 363–383). Cambridge, MA: Academic Press.

Haynes, C. (2019). *I was put in a school isolation booth more than 240 times*. Retrieved from: https://www.bbc.com/news/education-47898657

Holt-Lunstad, J., Smith, T. B., Baker, M., Harris, T., & Stephenson, D. (2015). Loneliness and social isolation as risk factors for mortality: A meta-analytic review. *Perspectives on Psychological Science*, 10(2), 227–237.

Kinchin, I., & Doran, C. M. (2018). The cost of youth suicide in Australia. *International Journal of Environmental Research and Public Health*, 15(4), 672.

Moieni, M., & Eisenberger, N. I. (2018). Effects of inflammation on social processes and implications for health. *Annals of the New York Academy of Sciences*, 1428(1), 5–13.

Olcoń, K., Kim, Y., & Gulbas, L. E. (2017). Sense of belonging and youth suicidal behaviors: What do communities and schools have to do with it? *Social Work in Public Health*, 32(7), 432–442.

Putnick, D. L., Bornstein, M. H., Lansford, J. E., Malone, P. S., Pastorelli, C., Skinner, A. T., Sorbring, E., Tapanya, S., Tirado, L. M. U., Zelli, A., Alampay, L. P., Al-Hassan, S. M., Bacchini, D., Bombi, A. S., Chang, L., Deater-Deckard, K., Di Giunta, L., Dodge, K. A., & Oburu, P. (2015). Perceived mother and father acceptance-rejection predict four unique aspects of child adjustment across nine countries. *Journal of Child Psychology and Psychiatry*, 56(8), 923–932.

Slavich, G. M. (2020). Social safety theory: A biologically based evolutionary perspective on life stress, health, and behavior. *Annual Review of Clinical Psychology*, 16, 265–295. Retrieved from: https://doi.org/10.1146/annurev-clinpsy-032816-045159

Steger, M. F., & Kashdan, T. B. (2009). Depression and everyday social activity, belonging, and well-being. *Journal of Counseling Psychology*, 56(2), 289–300.

Williams, K. D., Cheung, C. K., & Choi, W. (2000). Cyberostracism: Effects of being ignored over the internet. *Journal of Personality and Social Psychology*, 79(5), 748–762.

Williams, K. D., & Jarvis, B. (2006). Cyberball: A program for use in research on interpersonal ostracism and acceptance. *Behavior Research Methods*, 38(1), 174–180.

Wyman, P. A., Pickering, T. A., Pisani, A. R., Rulison, K., Schmeelk-Cone, K., Hartley, C., Gould, M., Caine, E. D., LoMurray, M., Brown, C. H., & Valente, T. W. (2019). Peer-adult network structure and suicide attempts in 38 high schools: Implications for network-informed suicide prevention. *Journal of Child Psychology and Psychiatry*, 60(10), 1065–1075.

CHAPTER 5

Bakker, D., & Rickard, N. (2018). Engagement in mobile phone app for self-monitoring of emotional wellbeing predicts changes in mental health: Mood-Prism. *Journal of Affective Disorders*, 227, 432–442.

Beard, K. W. (2002). Internet addiction: Current status and implications for employees. *Journal of Employment Counseling*, 39(1), 2–11.

Bonetti, L., Campbell, M. A., & Gilmore, L. (2010). The relationship of loneliness and social anxiety with children's and adolescents' online communication. *Cyberpsychology, Behavior, and Social Networking*, 13(3), 279–285.

Christofaro, D. G. D., De Andrade, S. M., Mesas, A. E., Fernandes, R. A., & Farias Junior, J. C. (2016). Higher screen time is associated with overweight, poor dietary habits and physical inactivity in Brazilian adolescents, mainly among girls. *European Journal of Sport Science*, 16(4), 498–506.

Drago, E. (2015). The effect of technology on face-to-face communication. *Elon Journal of Undergraduate Research in Communications*, 6(1), 13–19.

Duch, H., Fisher, E. M., Ensari, I., Font, M., Harrington, A., Taromino, C., Yip, J., & Rodriguez, C. (2013). Association of screen time use and language development in Hispanic toddlers: A cross-sectional and longitudinal study. *Clinical Pediatrics*, 52(9), 857–865.

Erdoğan, Y. (2008). Exploring the relationships among internet usage, internet attitudes and loneliness of Turkish adolescents. *Cyberpsychology: Journal of Psychosocial Research on Cyberspace*, 2(2), article 4.

Goodman-Deane, J., Mieczakowski, A., Johnson, D., Goldhaber, T., & Clarkson, P. J. (2016). The impact of communication technologies on life and relationship satisfaction. *Computers in Human Behavior*, 57, 219–229.

Jones, Q. (1997). Virtual-communities, virtual settlements & cyber-archaeology: A theoretical outline. *Journal of Computer-Mediated Communication*, 3(3), JCMC331.

Khosravi, P., Rezvani, A., & Wiewiora, A. (2016). The impact of technology on older adults' social isolation. *Computers in Human Behavior*, 63, 594–603. Retrieved from: https://doi.org/10.1016/j.chb.2016.05.092; https://www.sciencedirect.com/science/article/pii/S0747563216304289

Kircaburun, K., & Griffiths, M. D. (2018). Instagram addiction and the Big Five of personality: The mediating role of self-liking. *Journal of Behavioral Addictions*, 7(1), 158–170.

Kushlev, K., & Dunn, E. W. (2019). Smartphones distract parents from cultivating feelings of connection when spending time with their children. *Journal of Social and Personal Relationships*, 36(6), 1619–1639.

Kuss, D. J., & Griffiths, M. D. (2011). Online social networking and addiction – A review of the psychological literature. *International Journal of Environmental Research and Public Health*, 8(9), 3528–3552.

Lauricella, A. R., Wartella, E., & Rideout, V. J. (2015). Young children's screen time: The complex role of parent and child factors. *Journal of Applied Developmental Psychology*, 36, 11–17.

Mares, M. L., & Pan, Z. (2013). Effects of sesame street: A meta-analysis of children's learning in 15 countries. *Journal of Applied Developmental Psychology*, 34(3), 140–151.

McDaniel, B. T., & Radesky, J. S. (2018). Technoference: Longitudinal associations between parent technology use, parenting stress, and child behavior problems. *Pediatric Research*, 84(2), 210–218.

McMillan, D. W., & Chavis, D. M. (1986). Sense of community: A definition and theory. *Journal of Community Psychology*, 14(1), 6–23.

Morris, M. E., Kathawala, Q., Leen, T. K., Gorenstein, E. E., Guilak, F., DeLeeuw, W., & Labhard, M. (2010). Mobile therapy: Case study evaluations of a cell phone application for emotional self-awareness. *Journal of Medical Internet Research*, 12(2), e10.

Orben, A., & Baukney-Przybylski, A. K. (2018). Screens, teens and psychological well-being: Evidence from three time-use diary studies. *Psychological Science*, 30(5), 682–696.

Parent, J., Sanders, W., & Forehand, R. (2016). Youth screen time and behavioral health problems: The role of sleep duration and disturbances. *Journal of Developmental and Behavioral Pediatrics: JDBP*, 37(4), 277–284.

Pittman, M., & Reich, B. (2016). Social media and loneliness: Why an Instagram picture may be worth more than a thousand Twitter words. *Computers in Human Behavior*, 62, 155–167.

Putnam, R. D. (2000). *Bowling alone: The collapse and revival of American community.* New York, NY: Simon and Schuster.

Richards, R., McGee, R., Williams, S. M., Welch, D., & Hancox, R. J. (2010). Adolescent screen time and attachment to parents and peers. *Archives of Pediatrics & Adolescent Medicine*, 164(3), 258–262.

Sheldon, P., Rauschnabel, P. A., Antony, M. G., & Car, S. (2017). A cross-cultural comparison of Croatian and American social network sites: Exploring cultural differences in motives for Instagram use. *Computers in Human Behavior*, 75, 643–651.

Stepanikova, I., Nie, N. H., & He, X. (2010). Time on the Internet at home, loneliness, and life satisfaction: Evidence from panel time-diary data. *Computers in Human Behavior*, 26(3), 329–338.

Strouse, G. A., O'Doherty, K., & Troseth, G. L. (2013). Effective coviewing: Preschoolers' learning from video after a dialogic questioning intervention. *Developmental Psychology*, 49(12), 2368–2382.

Tandon, P. S., Zhou, C., Sallis, J. F., Cain, K. L., Frank, L. D., & Saelens, B. E. (2012). Home environment relationships with children's physical activity, sedentary time, and screen time by socioeconomic status. *International Journal of Behavioral Nutrition and Physical Activity*, 9(1), 88.

Turkle, S. (2011). *Alone together: Why we expect more from technology and less from each other.* New York, NY: Basic Books.

Weiser, E. B. (2001). The functions of internet use and their social and psychological consequences. *Cyberpsychology & Behavior*, 4(6), 723–743.

Yang, C. C. (2016). Instagram use, loneliness, and social comparison orientation: Interact and browse on social media, but don't compare. *Cyberpsychology, Behavior, and Social Networking*, 19(12), 703–708.

CHAPTER 6

Brotherton, D. C., & Gude, R (2020). Social control and the gang: Lessons from the legalization of street gangs in Ecuador. *Critical Criminology*. Retrieved from: https://doi.org/10.1007/s10612-020-09505-5

Campelo, N., Oppetit, A., Neau, F., Cohen, D., & Bronsard, G. (2018). Who are the European youths willing to engage in radicalisation? A multidisciplinary review of their psychological and social profiles. *European Psychiatry*, 52, 1–14. Retrieved from: http://dx.doi.org/10.1016/j.eurpsy.2018.03.001

Curry, D. (2004). Gangs: A high price to pay for belonging. *Criminal Justice Matters*, 55, 14–15.

Federal Bureau of Investigation. (2011). *National gang threat assessment*. Retrieved from: https://www.fbi.gov/stats-services/publications/2011-national-gang-threat-assessment

Hogg, M. A., Meehan, C., & Farquharson, J. (2010). The solace of radicalism: Self-uncertainty and group identification in the face of threat. *Journal of Experimental Social Psychology*, 46(6), 1061–1066.

Itaoui, R., & Dunn, K. (2017). Media representations of racism and spatial mobility: Young Muslim (un) belonging in a post-Cronulla riot Sutherland. *Journal of Intercultural Studies*, 38(3), 315–332.

Kruglanski, A., Belanger, J., Gelfand, M., & Sheveland, A. (2014). The psychology of radicalization and deradicalization: How significance quest impacts violent extremism. *Political Psychology*, 35(1), 69–93. Retrieved from: https://doi.org/10.1111/pops.12163

Kühne, T. (2010). *Belonging and genocide: Hitler's community, 1918–1945*. New Haven, CT: Yale University Press.

Lenzi, M., Sharkey, J. D., Wroblewski, A., Furlong, M. J., & Santinello, M. (2019). Protecting youth from gang membership: Individual and school-level emotional competence. *Journal of Community Psychology*, 47(3), 563–578.

Lyons-Padilla, S., Gelfand, M. J., Mirahmadi, H., Farooq, M., & Van Egmond, M. (2015). Belonging nowhere: Marginalization & radicalization risk among Muslim immigrants. *Behavioral Science & Policy*, 1(2), 1–12.

Monbiot, G. (2017). *Out of the wreckage: A new politics for an age of crisis*. Brooklyn, NY: Verso Books.

Nichols, S. L. (2006). Teachers' and students' beliefs about student belonging in one middle school. *The Elementary School Journal*, 106(3), 255–271.

Riley, K. (2020, January). *How to create schools which are places of welcome and belonging for all*. Keynote presented at the 33rd International Congress for School Effectiveness and Improvement (ICSEI). Marrakesh, Morocco.

Robinson, B., Frye, E. M., & Bradley, L. J. (1997). Cult affiliation and disaffiliation: Implications for counseling. *Counseling and Values*, 41(2), 166–173.

Roffey, S. (2013). Inclusive and exclusive belonging: The impact on individual and community wellbeing. *Educational and Child Psychology*, 30(1), 38–49.

Van Ngo, H., Calhoun, A., Worthington, C., Pyrch, T., & Este, D. (2017). The unravelling of identities and belonging: Criminal gang involvement of youth from immigrant families. *Journal of International Migration and Integration*, 18, 63–84. Retrieved from: https://doi.org/10.1007/s12134-015-0466-5

Zhang, K. (2017). The cultic phenomenon of youths: An educational perspective. *EC Psychology and Psychiatry*, 2(3), 106–111.

CHAPTER 7

Allen, K. A., Kern, M. L., Vella-Brodrick, D., & Waters, L. (2017). School values: A comparison of academic motivation, mental health promotion, and school belonging with student achievement. *The Educational and Developmental Psychologist*, 34(1), 31–47. Retrieved from: doi:10.1017/edp.2017.5

Allen, K. A., Kern, M. L., Vella-Brodrick, D., Waters, L., & Hattie, J. (2018). What schools need to know about belonging: A meta-analysis. *Educational Psychology Review*, 30(1), 1–34. Retrieved from: https://doi.org/10.1007/s10648-016-9389-8

Allen, K. A., Kern, P., Vella-Brodrick, D., & Waters, L. (2018). Understanding the priorities of Australian secondary schools through an analysis of their mission and vision statements. *Educational Administration Quarterly*, 54(2), 249–274.

Allen, K. A., Vella-Brodrick, D., & Waters, L. (2017). School belonging and the role of social and emotional competencies in fostering an adolescent's sense of connectedness to their school. In E. Frydenberg, A. J. Martin, & R. J. Collie (Eds.), *Social and emotional Learning in Australia and the Asia-Pacific: Perspectives, programs and approaches* (1st ed., pp. 83–99). Singapore: Springer. Retrieved from: https://doi.org/10.1007/978-981-10-3394-0_5

Amichai-Hamburger, Y., Wainapel, G., & Fox, S. (2002). "On the internet no one knows I'm an introvert": Extroversion, neuroticism, and Internet interaction. *Cyberpsychology & Behavior*, 5(2), 125–128.

Aron, A., Aron, E. N., & Smollan, D. (1992). Inclusion of other in the self scale and the structure of interpersonal closeness. *Journal of Personality and Social Psychology*, 63(4), 596–612.

Aron, A., Melinat, E., Aron, E. N., Vallone, R. D., & Bator, R. J. (1997). The experimental generation of interpersonal closeness: A procedure and some preliminary findings. *Personality and Social Psychology Bulletin*, 23(4), 363–377.

Baumeister, R. F., Brewer, L. E., Tice, D. M., & Twenge, J. M. (2007). Thwarting the need to belong: Understanding the interpersonal and inner effects of social exclusion. *Social and Personality Psychology Compass*, 1(1), 506–520.

Baumeister, R. F., DeWall, C. N., Ciarocco, N. J., & Twenge, J. M. (2005). Social exclusion impairs self-regulation. *Journal of Personality and Social Psychology*, 88(4), 589–604.

Baumeister, R. F., & Leary, M. R. (1995). The need to belong: Desire for interpersonal attachments as a fundamental human motivation. *Psychological Bulletin*, 117(3), 497–529.

Becvar, D., & Becvar, R. (2000). *Family therapy: A systematic integration*. Needham Heights, MA: Allen & Bacon.

Bowles, T., & Scull, J. (2018). The centrality of connectedness: A conceptual synthesis of attending, belonging, engaging and flowing. *Journal of Psychologists and Counsellors in Schools*, 29(1), 3–21.

Burgess, L. G., Riddell, P. M., Fancourt, A., & Murayama, K. (2018). The influence of social contagion within education: A motivational perspective. *Mind, Brain, and Education*, 12(4), 164–174.

Cacioppo, S., Capitanio, J. P., & Cacioppo, J. T. (2014). Toward a neurology of loneliness. *Psychological Bulletin*, 140(6), 1464–1504.

Cacioppo, S., Grippo, A. J., London, S., Goossens, L., & Cacioppo, J. T. (2015). Loneliness: Clinical import and interventions. *Perspectives on Psychological Science*, 10(2), 238–249.

Correa-Velez, I., Gifford, S. M., & Barnett, A. G. (2010). Longing to belong: Social inclusion and wellbeing among youth with refugee backgrounds in the first three years in Melbourne, Australia. *Social Science & Medicine*, 71(8), 1399–1408.

Cuervo, H., & Cook, J. (2018). Formations of belonging in Australia: The role of nostalgia in experiences of time and place. *Population, Space and Place*, 25(5), e2214.

Davis, K. (2012). Friendship 2.0: Adolescents' experiences of belonging and self-disclosure online. *Journal of Adolescence*, 35(6), 1527–1536.

De Dreu, C. K., & Kret, M. E. (2016). Oxytocin conditions intergroup relations through upregulated in-group empathy, cooperation, conformity, and defense. *Biological Psychiatry*, 79(3), 165–173.

Devine-Wright, P., Price, J., & Leviston, Z. (2015). My country or my planet? Exploring the influence of multiple place attachments and ideological beliefs upon climate change attitudes and opinions. *Global Environmental Change*, 30, 68–79. Retrieved from: https://doi.org/10.1016/j.gloenvcha.2014.10.012

Donovan, R. J., James, R., Jalleh, G., & Sidebottom, C. (2006). Implementing mental health promotion: The act-belong-commit mentally healthy WA campaign in Western Australia. *International Journal of Mental Health Promotion*, 8(1), 33–42.

Ferguson, M. A., & Branscombe, N. R. (2010). Collective guilt mediates from effect of beliefs about global warming on willingness to engage in mitigation behavior. *Journal of Environmental Psychology*, 30, 135–142. Retrieved from: https://doi.org/10.1016/j.jenvp.2009.11.010

Fujii, T., Schug, J., Nishina, K., Takahashi, T., Okada, H., & Takagishi, H. (2016). Relationship between salivary oxytocin levels and generosity in preschoolers. *Scientific Reports*, 6(1), 1–7.

Gautam, A. (2019). The monstrous other: Adam Goodes and the colonial legacy of 'terra nullius'. *Social Alternatives*, 38(4), 16. (Abstract). Retrieved from: https://search.informit.com.au/documentSummary;dn=002198709234920;res=IELAPA

Gehlbach, H., Brinkworth, M. E., King, A. M., Hsu, L. M., McIntyre, J., & Rogers, T. (2016). Creating birds of similar feathers: Leveraging similarity to improve teacher–student relationships and academic achievement. *Journal of Educational Psychology*, 108(3), 342–352. Retrieved from: https://doi.org/10.1037/edu0000042

Gere, J., & MacDonald, G. (2010). An update of the empirical case for the need to belong. *Journal of Individual Psychology*, 66(1), 93–115.

Heider, F. (1958). *The psychology of interpersonal relations*. New York, NY: Psychology Press.

hooks, b. (2009). *Reel to real: Race, class and sex at the movies*. Abingdon, UK: Routledge.

Kandel, D. B. (1978). Homophily, selection, and socialization in adolescent friendships. *American Journal of Sociology*, 84(2), 427–436.

Keyes, E. F., & Kane, C. F. (2004). Belonging and adapting: Mental health of Bosnian refugees living in the United States. *Issues in Mental Health Nursing*, 25(8), 809–831.

Leary, M. R., & Allen, A. B. (2011). Belonging motivation: Establishing, maintaining, and repairing relational value. In D. Dunning (Ed.), *Frontiers of social psychology. Social motivation* (pp. 37–55). New York, NY: Psychology Press.

Maner, J. K., DeWall, C. N., Baumeister, R. F., & Schaller, M. (2007). Does social exclusion motivate interpersonal reconnection? Resolving the "porcupine problem". *Journal of Personality and Social Psychology*, 92(1), 42–55.

Mauro, M. (2016). Transcultural football. Trajectories of belonging among immigrant youth. *Soccer & Society*, 17(6), 882–897.

Mello, Z. R., Mallett, R. K., Andretta, J. R., & Worrell, F. C. (2012). Stereotype threat and school belonging in adolescents from diverse racial/ethnic backgrounds. *Journal of At-Risk Issues*, 17(1), 9–14.

Minuchin, S. (1974). Therapeutic implications of a structural approach. In *Families and Family Therapy* (pp. 96–97). London: Tavistock.

Moore, K., & McElroy, J. C. (2012). The influence of personality on Facebook usage, wall postings, and regret. *Computers in Human Behavior*, 28(1), 267–274.

Mother Theresa. (1979). *Transcript of Mother Teresa's acceptance speech, held on 10 December 1979 in the Aula of the University of Oslo, Norway*. Retrieved from: https://www.nobelprize.org/prizes/peace/1979/teresa/26200-mother-teresa-acceptance-speech-1979/

Ryan, R. M., & Deci, E. L. (2000). Self-determination theory and the facilitation of intrinsic motivation, social development, and well-being. *American Psychologist*, 55(1), 68–78.

Seidman, G. (2013). Self-presentation and belonging on Facebook: How personality influences social media use and motivations. *Personality and Individual Differences*, 54(3), 402–407.

Swim, J. K., Stern, P. C., Doherty, T. J., Clayton, S., Reser, J. P., Weber, E. U., et al. (2011). Psychology's contributions to understanding and addressing global climate change. *American Psychologist*, 66, 241e250. Retrieved from: http://dx.doi.org/10.1037/a0023220

Uzzell, D., Pol, E., & Badenas, D. (2002). Place identification, social cohesion, and environmental sustainability. *Environment and Behavior*, 34, 26–53.

Yeager, D. S., & Walton, G. M. (2011). Social-psychological interventions in education: They're not magic. *Review of Educational Research*, 81(2), 267–301.